"I believe
be both in
closer to (... urther forward in their
spiritual journey through life!"

—Bishop Mark Steven Filkey, West Coast World Outreach Church, Stockton, CA

"This book is loaded with inspiring stories and thought-provoking poetry. Through Shadoew's willingness to be transparent, the world has yet another fine, firsthand account of the faithfulness of God in the life of one who has chosen to trust him. *From the Father's Heart* is a powerful, timeless book. An excellent read."

—Kristle Murden

"Simply inspirational! *From the Father's Heart* will cause you to breathe again. Grab yourself a hot cup of tea and enjoy!"

—Pastor Alvin Fruga, Presence Theater Church, Owasso, OK

"*From the Father's Heart* is an expression of intimacy and spiritual insight. The poem *Dance with Me* and *All of Me,* as well as all the other writings, carry the depth of spiritual intelligence and taps into desperation for God. The pages of this book will enhance your capacity to achieve a level of greater worship."

—Bishop Shaun D. Cooper Sr., New Creation Family Church, Shreveport, LA

“The words in this book are inspirational and directly from the Father’s heart. This work will challenge you to come closer to God and to experience His unconditional love and favor. The author’s intimate relationship with Jesus comes through as the words pierce your heart, and you will know that you have heard from the Father.”

—Helen Trowbridge, Trowbridge Ministries

“From the Father’s Heart is an interactive experience that will motivate you to continue to seek His Heart every day. In a time when people are yearning for a deep, meaningful encounter with God, Shadoew has captured the wisdom and knowledge of the Father in the form of prophetic poems. This is truly a gift for all who seek Him.

—Pastor Isaac O. Rangel, Founder and Senior Pastor of City on a Hill, Corpus Christi, Texas

“Riveting. You can hear God speaking to you as you read this book!”

—Cheryl Boggs

“From the Father’s Heart reassures you of who you are in Christ; to know that He is with you always, and that He will never leave you alone. This will be a book that you will keep on your nightstand and share and read with your children and others.”

—Angella Harris, Children’s Ministry, Restoration Ministries, Visalia, CA

FROM THE FATHER'S HEART

FROM THE FATHER'S HEART

A situational poetic glimpse into relationship with God

Shadoew Rose Terrell

Tate Publishing & *Enterprises*

Published by Tate Publishing & Enterprises, LLC
127 E. Trade Center Terrace | Mustang, Oklahoma 73064 USA
1.888.361.9473 | www.tatepublishing.com

Tate Publishing is committed to excellence in the publishing industry. The company reflects the philosophy established by the founders, based on Psalm 68:11,
"The Lord gave the word and great was the company of those who published it."

Cover design by Blake Brasor
Interior design by Stefanie Rane

Published in the United States of America

ISBN: 978-1-61739-022-7
1. Poetry, Inspirational & Religious
2. Religion, Christian Life, Inspirational
10.08.20

Dedication

It would only seem appropriate to dedicate this inspirational poetic book to the One who inspired me to write it, God the Father.

God, to You be all glory and honor. Who is like You? There is no one. I dedicate these writings that are comprised within this book to You. I hope that these words do what You intend for them to do; penetrate the hearts of many. It is my desire You be glorified and that men, women and children of all ages, color and backgrounds would be drawn to You with an aspiration for a closer relationship with the God who created them.

I pray You are pleased with what I have done with what You have given me. You are more than awesome. There are times I cannot find words to describe or give an accurate account of who You are. You are too much! You are too great! A glimpse into a small facet of You is sometimes overwhelming, but please do not stop expressing or revealing Yourself to me. The relationship You have drawn me into is beautiful, intriguing and supernaturally mysterious. I cannot live without Your instruction, direction and wisdom; for it is I who am in desperate need of you.

I also dedicate this poetic book to my mother, Johnnie Mae Morris. Mom, you were the first person who introduced me to God as a child. You have always lived your life as a woman of God. You instilled in me the difference between right and wrong. You taught your children in the ways of the Lord and you have done well. I remember those Sunday mornings at Uncle Wilburn's church; they were so much fun and so exciting. I inherited God from you, and that is the greatest gift you could have ever given me. It is the most solid, sure and sound thing I possess in my life. You are an exceptionally strong person and yet so sweet, loving and tender in your heart. You are my mother, an awesome woman and a great friend. I love you with all my heart; your seventh child.

Acknowledgments

I could not have arrived where I am today without the support and boost of some awesome applauders in my life. I have had some wonderful people who have persuaded and encouraged me along my journey. There are many vital people in my life that I do not have room on the pages to mention, but please know that I love and appreciate all of you and hold you dear in my heart. To these whom I acknowledge, I do so because you have played a significant role in influencing the direction of my life. No one is most or least important according to placement; this is simply the order in which I thought of you.

Bishop Shawn Cooper, I can hear your words in the back of my mind, saying, "You need to finish your book, Rose! You need to finish your book." I could hear you almost every day. Thanks for being that voice that always reminded me that I have something of importance to accomplish. Maybe now I can get you out of my mind. Well, it was just a thought. I have two more books to publish and I still hear those prophetic words ringing as clear as the day you spoke them to me, "One hour a day Rose; invest one hour a day in what God has given you." Sometimes I spent an hour, sometimes two, sometimes it was all day and now here I am. Thank you for being a vital instrument.

To my sister Charle, my best friend, you have always believed in me. You have always maintained the faith that I could do anything and believed that

I could. You always intrigued me with that disposition. When I struggled to believe in myself, I heard the faith in your heart, as you would always speak the opposite of what I would say. I would tell you, "I can't do that!" you would say, "Girl, yes you can; you can do anything." You have been one of my greatest supporters. You have been on my side, cheering for me all along the way through every effort in my life. I love you so much! I remember you! My beautiful little sister, you will never know the impact you have made in my life. Thank you for inspiring me to believe that I can really spread my wings, ride on the breath of God, and truly fly.

Bishop Robert E. Hooks, my pastor, friend and brother, you have been a constant voice of God in my life: prophet, preacher, teacher, pastor, man of the living God. You are an expression of God's heart. I have never seen you waiver in your dedication to deliberately point us all to God through Jesus Christ. You have made every effort to bring us into the knowledge of who God is, who we are to Him and in Him that we may acquire a tangible and revelatory relationship. By this, I am provoked with a fervent desire to capture the essence of who He is. It is such an honor and a privilege to sit under your leadership. I have been shaped, sculpted, rebuked, corrected, and revolutionized by the revelation God has given to you. Thank you for your commitment to God. I am blessed because of it. Thank you for the sacrifices you have made; I am a benefactor of them. Thank you so much for always teaching God's truth. It keeps me safely embraced in the arms of God. You truly are my Father's son.

To my husband, friend and lover, Clarence Terrell Jr., you delicious and lovely thing! Oh! You are the most beautiful person I know. Your passion is my necessary daily dose of love. I am addicted to it! God created something wonderful and precious when He formed you. You have taught me how to love, laugh, and shed a few tears, yet there isn't anything in my life with you that I would trade. Your kindness and gentle spirit captured my heart the first day I dined with you so many years ago. I was yours forever and am still! The generosity of your heart still bewilders me. I am blown away by how gracious and kind you are. Thank you for your support in everything I do, whether I succeed or whether I fail. You have relentlessly encouraged me to do what God has gifted me to do. You have encouraged me to become a more beautiful person within by allowing the Holy Spirit to have full reign in my life. I have learned much from you. You have taught your wife well. Thank you for your patience and tolerance with me. I know that I am not always easy. I am so thankful for you and grateful to God that you have found me. (Smile) When a man finds…

Table of Contents

Foreword

Over the last fifteen years, Clarence and Shadoew Terrell have served faithfully as associate pastors at Restoration Ministries Visalia, California. As a couple, their lifestyle—in both word and deed—has a lasting impact on our congregation and city. Clarence and Shadoew effectively convey the message of the Gospel. I am privileged to pastor them and have such gifts in our ministry.

One Sunday afternoon our staff of pastors decided to fellowship at a restaurant. As we ordered dinner, I noticed Shadoew's frequent glance at her watch. She was engaged in a conversation so I inquired of her husband Clarence; an amazing man, if she had a previous engagement. His reply pleasantly caught me off guard. He said, "Every day at a certain time Shadoew is in prayer. She refuses to allow anyone or anything to interfere with her prayer time."

Reflecting on that day which was many years ago, it does not surprise me that she would have a dedicated notebook to capture those precious moments. I was blessed to know that she refused to allow any interpose that would hinder her committed time spent with the Father. This attitude is priceless with any believer. Shadoew reminded me of a little girl that could hardly wait to talk with someone she loved and missed. I concluded after speaking with her on many occasions that this was exactly what was taking place in her heart.

The uniqueness of the prayers, songs and devotion to write poetry unto God is refreshing and thought provoking. This book is her world of personal devotion that certainly gives entry into Shadoew's heart. I pray that everyone that reads this book, both young and old, refuse to give up the little girl or boy within. I pray that we all continue to see our Father as stronger, bigger, mightier, loving and full of forgiveness more than anyone else. Father, allow the readers of this book to stick out their chest and boast about what comes *From the Father's Heart.*

Because she lives for the pleasure of pleasing the Father and treasures every nuance in her experience with God, this book is very unique. Shadoew has found a treasure of wealth to draw from in the devotional commitment of hearing from the Lord. I personally want to thank Shadoew for sharing with us and giving us entry into her most prized possession, her time spent with the Father. May this book provoke all to spend more time in prayer. The results of spending time with the Father will be encouragement and strength. *From the Father's Heart* is a wonderful reality.

—Bishop Robert E. Hooks, Founder and Senior Pastor, Restoration Ministries, Visalia, CA

Introduction

When I was a child, I loved reading books and enjoyed writing the reports that accompanied them. It was stimulating. I began writing mini stories, and by the time I was a teen, I wrote poetry that I considered "situational." It usually sprung from an occurrence in my life or someone else's. I was always able to lay ink on paper in such a way that it described my thoughts with clarity and adequately articulated my unspoken words. I enjoyed it immensely! Little did I know that God had touched me with a very, very small portion of His creativity.

From The Father's Heart is a collection of songs, hymns, poetry and sayings that were inspired by the Spirit of God from situations and circumstances that have occurred in my life as well as others. From these issues in and throughout life, God has inspired me with the words that illuminate the poetic expressions on the pages of this book.

These poems are what I call "situational poetry." A short synopsis briefly describes the situation that occurred and what the Spirit of the Lord inspired me to write in that particular situation. God has always been here for me. He is always here to instruct, guide, aim, point, encourage, inspire and even rebuke me. His love and covering is really amazing. I am grateful for His grace and the sweet relationship He sustains between Him and I.

It is my deepest desire that those who would take the time to read the words carefully would find that God really does care about our lives and is desperately in love with each and every one of us. I hope these writings will encourage, uplift, strengthen and ignite the spirit of each person to run to God in pursuit of a closer relationship with Him. To find Him, to know who He is, and to attempt to understand the incomprehensible love He has for us all. The more you seek Him, the more you find Him; and the more you find Him, the more you understand He is so beyond who we are.

I hope this book will challenge many with renewed faith, if somewhere, in the twists and turns of life, faith has been lost, robbed, or surrendered to the trials that have been set before you. We have all endured some measure of something. Whether we are coming out or going in, we have been touched by something in life. Scripture teaches us that we have a Savior who has been touched with such likenesses; Jesus Christ. He understands all the challenges life presents and will help you to overcome every one of them if you call upon Him. He said, "I will never leave nor forsake you." It is His promise!

I am aware that this book is not for everyone because it is your choice to choose whether it is or it is not. It is, however, for those of us who understand that we all need God and need the encouragement, strength, and hope His Word provides. Is there anyone you know who does not need to be encouraged? It is for those of us who need to encourage ourselves yet encourage one another, to inspire ourselves and inspire one another. To know that God does hear and answers our prayers and there is assured hope in God through Christ Jesus. We must accept as truth what Scripture teaches and believe what God has said about Himself. We must believe what He has declared about us and who we are to Him and in Him. We must remember that all things work together for good to those who love God, to those who are called according to His magnificent purpose.

I Am

Prelude

Relationship with God is sometimes overwhelming, sometimes satisfying, sometimes frightening. God is beyond natural, yet He has manifested Himself by the natural things He has created. When you trust the invisible with the visible, the unseen with the seen, you must learn how to trust God in order to fellowship with Him; He who is tangible yet invisible. Yes! I declare to you, you can unequivocally feel Him. No! It is not *imaginary*. He is beyond your reality, the reality of what you have learned and comprehended in all the earth. God is spirit. Those that worship Him must worship Him in spirit and truth according to His own Word.

I am always wowed when God shares Himself with me. For who am I that He would consider me for anything? Yet He loves me desperately, passionately, and sacrificially, as revealed in His Son, Jesus Christ. One day after concluding my fellowship with God, this is what the Lord shared with me about Him.

I took of Myself,
Wrapped flesh around Myself,
Birthed Myself,
Walked upon the earth Myself,
Sacrificed Myself,

Reconciled the world through Myself,
Unto Myself,
Died Myself,
And yet raised Myself,
And ascended to My position in heaven,
Before I descended Myself,
Sent back the Spirit of the Holy Ghost.
This is Me, Myself,
To abide in you Myself!
Who am I if I am not the Great I Am?
I Am.

None Other

Prelude

There is no one else like God! He is awesome, He is wondrous, and He does the miraculous. He is incredible all by Himself, and He is always by our side to guide us, instruct us, teach us, and graciously and abundantly shower His love all over us. He declares to us who He is, that we may believe Him for the impossible, the improbable and the inconceivable. He has unfathomable riches to bestow upon His people. His mercy and grace is new and fresh every morning.

He is generous in His love and kindness toward us and will reward those who diligently seek to know Him. God is great, magnificent, incredible, and beautiful. He is the beginning and the end, there is nothing in between. There is no one to compare Him to, and there is nothing to compare Him with. He stands alone! He is God all by Himself! Self-sustained! He is the Creator of the universe and everything that is contained within. He alone holds all things together, and everything is sustained by Him. Who is like God; the wonder of my soul! No one!

I am the God of all creation!
The Bright and Morning Star!
The Alpha and the Omega!

The Beginning and the End!
The Great I Am!
There is none other like Me,
No one beside Me,
And none to compare Me with!
I am the Lilly of the Valley!
I lift and set the sun and moon in its place!
The stars radiate from My Glory!

I created you!
You are the one I formed; you are the
workmanship of My hands!
I am the One who overshadows you,
Takes care of you,
Hears your cries and knows what is in your tears!
I am the One who loves you the most,
Carries your best interest in My heart!
There is no one who loves you like Me!
Jealously, passionately, intensely and constantly!
I know the plans I made for your life!
A good and expected finish!

For I am God!
And there is none, none other like Me!

There is none!
No not one!

Courage

Prelude

Has the Lord ever just dropped something in your spirit to remind you of who you are or *whose* you are? Has He ever reminded you of who He is? God will cause your heart to grab a hold of the courage you need to put one foot in front of the other and keep moving? Sometimes you need to be reminded of who He is and who you are in Him, especially when your situation or set of circumstances is speaking contrary to the Word of the Lord in your life. This was one of those poems that God just dropped in my spirit to remind me that I belong to Him and that He is truly an awesome God.

Child of Destiny,
Hear and do listen.
I promised you that I would never
leave you nor forsake you,
I would never let you down.
For you are My crown and glory,
An inheritance unto Myself.
You are my loved!

You are created in My image to show
the expression of My attributes,
To represent the character and
conduct of Me in the earth,
To expose My goodness, kindness, and
love to a world who knows Me not.
There is no other that is fashioned like you.
You are a peculiar one.
You are Mine!

Know that I will always be here for you.
For wherever your here may be,
That is where I am!
Be of good courage!

Come Here

Prelude

In God's written Word, He has revealed His love, heart, thoughts, and His desire for relationship with His creation. Throughout relationship with God, He is constantly unveiling His will and desire to be known. To know Him requires all that you are and demands all your trust in who He says He is. He wants all and nothing less than all! He is not a part-time God attempting to involve you in a part-time relationship. He is a full-time God who desires a full-time relationship with you and me. He wants everything because He has given everything and withheld nothing. Therefore, He is consistent at requesting you to "come" that you may know and be known.

I've shared My heart with you,
My love with you,
My mind and thoughts with you.
Give me all that you are.
I want all of you.
Not pieces or parts, but all that you are.

There is no one who loves you greater than I.
There is no one that cares deeper for you than Me.
No not one!
I am love expressed!
Who can rescue you from out of
the eye of any storm?
Who can deliver you and give you
favor with wicked men?
Who can cause things to be; that
were not, for your good?

With whom am I to be compared?
Who is like the Lord of Hosts?
I am like no one.
I stand alone.
And I alone am God.
Give Me all of you!

Only Believe

Prelude

It was probably about five thirty in the morning, and I was driving on the freeway en route to work, crying and praying about my unaccomplished dreams and aspirations for my life. I was expressing to the Lord my disappointments due to loss of time and wondering how I could ever fulfill what I had hoped. As I was crying and driving that early morning, I wrote down these words that I heard sang in my spirit.

What an awesome God I serve! He is not limited by my time restraints. He can take an unfulfilled dream you have been working on for twenty years and cause you to excel in less than five. When you think it is over, He simply says, "Dust yourself off, get up, and get back into the race again. Be all I have created you to be! I have given you everything you need. You are My success story."

If you've given up hope and lost your dream,
The vision that you had is a faded memory,
And all you've hoped for you have not seen,
Just remember,
All things are possible to them who believe.

If fear has come and gripped your heart,
Caused you to stumble as you pursued who you are,
You didn't finish what you began to start,
Just remember,
All things are possible to them who believe.

So stir up your faith and dust yourself off.
Stand with the Word I have put inside your heart.
And pursue all that I, your God, have said you are.
And just remember,
All things are possible.

All things are possible!
Not just some things!
But all things are possible
To them who *believe.*

Going through the Fire

Prelude

This started out as this little grooving song I wrote. The more I sang it, the more I realized that the devil is not playing with our lives; he is out to kill, steal, and destroy whomever he can, whenever he can, by whatever means and methods he can articulate. The devil will strategically plan anything that will cause you to fall, trip, or stagger through life, killing your faith, hope, and dreams in God as well as in yourself. He was a murderer from the beginning and remains so until this day.

The Word of God teaches us that hope deferred makes the heart ill. If the devil is able to convince you not to hope, what can you look forward to? If he is able to deplete your faith, how will you ever believe God? We are in warfare. This is a fight, and this is a battle in which we must truly utilize our spiritual weaponry. You and I must suit up with battle gear. This is the battle gear that the Scripture commands us to put on—the whole armor of God. Get equipped!

I don't mind going through the fire;
I don't even mind going through the flame.
But what I do mind,
Is when they try to take my crown,
And steal my heavenly name.

I don't like that!
I must fight back!
I've got to use heavenly weapons of war.

The enemy tries to rob my spirit,
Steal all of my joy,
Kill the measure of faith my Father gives,
And leave me with hope no more.
I must stand up and fight,
For my right in Jesus Christ,
Be that valiant man of war,
And continue to remain faithfully on course.

Plant my feet and stand my ground:
Bind my loins with the truth,
Wear the breastplate of righteousness,
Dress my feet with the preparation of the gospel,
Beyond everything, take the shield
of faith, crush the fiery darts,
Take the helmet of salvation,
Seize the sword of the Spirit,
which is the Word of God,
Praying always in the Spirit with
all persistent determination.

I must speak those things that are not,
As though they were.
Say what God says,
Do what Jesus would do,
And be bold and fearless in the Spirit.
For I have everything to gain and nothing to lose.
If God is for me, and He is, who
can stand against me?
For I war on the winning side!

He Is Here

Prelude

As I think about the goodness of God, I am so grateful! There is not a day that goes by that I do not consider God's faithfulness, goodness, covering, and His love. He is so present in my life. It is not because of anything that I have done or given to Him. It is just because of who He is. God is so loving and kind and always willing to help me with any angle of my life. He answers questions I sometimes do not even know how to ask. He responds to what I need. He is faithful, faithful, faithful. He drew me unto Him that I may experience His compassion for me. Every day I am grateful and thankful to the only One who is constant. Nobody else can be God except God, and He is so good at being Himself. I am humbled.

I tell you of a life,
That I used to know.
And the story of the Glory,
That saved my empty soul.
I tell you of the grace,
That sweetly engulfed me.
And the pleasure in the treasure,
That only His love brings.

There was no one who considered me,
In the condition I was in.
Naked and ashamed of the things I had been in.
But God looked beyond my faults,
And He saw that I needed Him.
So He covered me with His love,
And began to teach me how to live.

He's not far away;
He's right here,
Ready to bend His ear,
For anyone who calls out to Him.
He will hear your cry,
Have mercy and heal your life,
Provide peace to a soul that aches within,
And forever settle you in Him.

God is not far away.
He is right here,
Ready and willing to bend His ear
For anyone who will call out to Him!

Do Right

Prelude

As long as you are living, there will be people in your life that do not meet your expectations. Whether they are your family, friends, girlfriend, boyfriend, husband, wife, children, siblings, or strangers; someone is going to disappoint you by their behavior or lack of appropriate conduct. You may hear words from someone whose heart is uncompassionate toward yours. You may find yourself standing alone when someone promised they would stand by your side. Life has its share of disappointments. They hurt badly. I know! But you must still obey God through all of the hurt and pain of your displeasure. God delights in obedience, and it is in obedience that God receives glory from our lives. It doesn't always feel good. It does not! But remember—there is a manifold blessing in the act of obedience. Be encouraged. God *will* take care of you.

People can talk about me,
Make scandal of my name,
Try to humiliate me,
And drag me through the shame.
Speak all manner of lies,
Never telling the truth,

To defame my character,
Just to see what I will do.
It doesn't matter what people say.
I've got to do right by the Father anyway.

Thought I had friends,
Standing by my side.
I looked to the left,
I searched on my right.
They lied, found none in sight.
Said that they loved me.
I had believed it was so.
Such evil done against me,
Had I only known?
It still doesn't matter what people do or say.
I've got to do right by the Father anyway.

I have discovered in this life,
That it doesn't matter what people say.
I must do right by the Father anyway.
It is His desire for me,
To long for the things of the King.
Pray for those that have wronged me,
Forgive them quickly,
That I may not be a stumbling block to any man,
And hinder the offering of Jesus's hand.
Understanding that we all have need,
Of the only One who can set us free.

It doesn't matter what people say.
I must do right by the Father anyway!

Resuscitation

Prelude

My husband had come home from the gym one morning and asked, "Honey, what's wrong? It seems like you have something on your mind." I told him I did. So he asked me to talk to him. As I began to share my heart with him, I explained that I did not have any passion or excitement for anything. He asked me at what point did I lose it? I told him I was in the process of evaluating that truth.

I explained that the most exciting time of my life was when I was creating something. I told him that as I looked over the last several years, I had no expression of the creative gifts that God has so blessed me with. I asked him to pray for me, and he prayed with me. I had been praying and asking the Lord, "What is going on with me? How am I not excited about life? God, help me restore my enthusiasm and passion." I said to the Lord, "I need You to talk to me! The only voice I want to hear right now is Yours. I need Your instruction and Your direction." There was a thought that came into my mind, and I went into my bedroom to write it down. As I began, this is what I heard from the Lord regarding what I had just shared with my husband. He is so faithful.

I can resuscitate your life,
With just one breath of Mine.
I can renew strength in you,
Revive the spirit I placed in you.
I am the breath you need,
To restore your dreams,
To reestablish the visions that I have given you,
And give you what is necessary
to follow them through.

I am the breath you need,
To restore your soul to Me,
And cause you to share My heart as you once did.
Remember where you once hid?
Under the shadow of My being,
Where I exposed to you secret things,
Things that you never knew,
Things that were just for you,
That which was between just you and me.

I am the breath you need.
Come and return to Me.
I can resuscitate your life,
With just one breath of Mine.
I am the breath you need.
Come to Me and breathe.

Protection

Prelude

When you consider who you are to God and really think about the provisions He has provided for you, it stirs your faith. When you consider your life and reflect on how God has protected and kept you, it continues to build your confidence in the only true and living God. You are confident and sure, knowing that if He has proved Himself thus far, He will not disappoint you now or in your future. You understand that nothing you receive is because of who you are; but solely because of who He is and what He has already accomplished through Christ Jesus. God has you and me covered. We must believe and trust Him.

God sits on the throne of heaven and oversees
the counsel of His will for your life.

Jesus Christ sits on the right hand of the
Father, making intersession for you.

The Holy Spirit, who is your Comforter,
leads you into all truth.

The ministering angels of the Lord fight
principalities of the air on your behalf.

And then God makes sure all things work
together for the good for those who love Him,

And for those who are called
according to His purpose.

If God be for us, tell me, who are
they that can stand against us?

Who are they?

Just for You and Me

Prelude

When you remember and consider what Christ did in order to reconcile us back to the Creator who so loves us, it is mindboggling to say the least. The suffering and incredible pain Christ endured, is incomprehensible to me. I cannot grasp, articulate, reason, or understand how Christ did what He did on our behalf. My mind cannot gather or collect a viable rational that will assist me in understanding this kind of love. I am acutely aware the Word reads, "For God so loved that He gave His only begotten Son." Unexplainable is the Word, who became Christ in the flesh, who was willing to endure such affliction and suffering. He was not accustomed to such anguish, for He was spirit. For the love of man, He wrapped Himself in flesh and suffered pain, hatred, torture, and finally murder in our stead. He took our place that we would not receive the wrath of God, thus opening the door for communication and relationship. My mind does not have the ability to expand that far. I am not talking about what a man did but what God Himself did for a people who had not considered Him. This is beyond a great act. This is enormous! Grab this with your mind…

God put on flesh, birthed Himself, sacrificed Himself and raised Himself for people who did not know Him, all because of His love for us. What kind of love would do this? I do not understand it in its totality. But I am grateful every day for the reconciliation to God through Christ. I am thankful that God had a plan for us and the Word agreed to become the answer.

He stretched His arms open wide;
The Father separated Himself as He cried,
"Father, why hast thou forsaken Me?"
As the wrath of God crushed Him beyond any.
My sins and the worlds separated Him,
And it pleased God to behold Him stricken.
So He bore my transgressions
along with all of our shame.
He hung on a rugged cross, guiltless, without blame.
He did it just for you and me.

They beat Him for our sake.
Slashes across His back He did undertake,
When He stepped down from above,
To perform the will of the Father's love,
For people who did not know,
That He was God wrapped in fleshly clothes.
In His truth He is revealed.
By His stripes we are healed.
He did this just for you and me.

In three days He rose from the grave.
God seated us with Him in heavenly places,
And blessed us in the heavenly realms,
With every spiritual blessing Christ held.
He gave us power and authority.

He has equipped us with everything we need.
He leads us through the dark as
well as through the light.
He directs our paths in His righteousness.
He did it just for you and me.
Christ.

Purpose

Prelude

Purpose is the reason for which you were born. It is the reason you were created. God holds your reason within Himself. It is only in God that you will discover the reason for your existence and live out your purpose. Outside of God you might find what you desire for your life. Inside of God you discover your true identity; the truth of who you are. What we desire is often in conflict with the will of God for our lives. God created us and knows every detail of our being. He knows what is good, and He knows what is not. We think we know what is best, but do we? We cannot see into the next moment, day, month, or year. He sees all and knows at all times what is before us. Therefore, He is an excellent guide to lead us through life, if we allow Him. You can spend so much time prepping and preparing yourself for what you desire to become and discover it is not your *true* purpose. Who God says you are and who you claim to be, are really two different people. One discovers and satisfies the reason for their existence, while the other attempts to satisfy the purpose they desire for themselves. This is the lesser of the two and results in not achieving the greatest life that can be lived. God wants you to live the greatest life possible in the purpose for which He created you. He will help you understand the mark you are to leave in the earth and the impact you are to make in the lives of men. There is a reason for everyone born under the sun. Yes, you must seek the Creator to understand the reason for which you were created. He alone holds your answer.

There is a time and reason for
everything under the sun.
An allotment of time has been given
to pursue the reason you live.
To fulfill and complete your
destiny before you expire.
And satisfy the reason for which you
have come into the earth.

A collection of moments comprise your life.
For every man born God alone knows
the reasons for his moments.
They are secure in the wisdom
and knowledge of God,
The purpose, the plan and the success of your life.

God must be the One you reach for.
He must be the One you seek out and discover.
In discovering Him, you discover yourself.
It is in Him you discover your truth,
and find your reason for being.

There are many things you may choose to become,
But is it the person God created you to be?
Will you be the one God wanted you to discover?
And uncover the expected end
God has laid out for you?

God delights in you being blessed,
exceptionally blessed!
Living in and pursuing the reason for which you are.
But who you are is found in God alone.
For He alone holds the course for your destiny,
And knows the purpose and reason for your life.

Eye Contact

Prelude

God's Word gives you the ability to capture a glimpse of who He is. It affords you the privileged opportunity to peek into a crevice in the mind of God. Our mortal mind attempts with great diligence to cultivate and intellectually process His will: way, delights, desires, hatred, wrath, love, kindness, tender mercy, grace, covering, protection, anger, devotion, and His faithfulness.

His Word affords you and me an opportunity to look through spectrums of truth to clarify who we are and discover our identity in Him. It simultaneously allows us to come into the knowledge of who He is as He unveils Himself before you and me. It is a matrix which establishes a peculiar journey of supernatural experiences, face-to-face with the many brilliant facets of His unchangeable person. A spirit-to-spirit intense relationship filled with passion, privilege, and power. It is an indescribable love affair with the Creator of all creation who delights in relationship with His children. It is here where you find yourself engaged in eye contact with God. He elevates your mind to a place that discovers the revelation of who He is and helps you perceive things as He sees them. Your eyes are fixed through His. You see through the eyes of God.

God has afforded you and me the opportunity to apprehend this—seeing through His eyes. Please, pause and take note. Post this to the walls of your mind and do not forget. The enemy despises your eye contact with God. He hates it! He hates your intimate relationship with Him. There is a pure disgust for your bond and unity with God. At every occasion the enemy will attempt to sweep your feet from beneath you. He will utilize whomever he can and whatever he can to distract you. He is deliberately calculating and will endlessly endeavor to force you to lose eye contact with the lover of your soul. His goal is to derail you from being in harmony and in melody with the heartbeat of God. Keep your eyes fixed on God. Fight to maintain your eye contact with Him!

The Word of God is God.
In His Word He has disclosed Himself,
Revealing mysteries of ancient days,
Set in place for modern time.

It is privileged information,
That is only revealed by His spirit.
Man within himself cannot grasp or comprehend it.
It is revealed by God through relationship with Him.

The Word gives life and is light.
It illuminates the mind and provides sight.
Sight into the unseen,
The other side of God's reality.

The Word adjust your vision to eclipse
the truth of what He sees,
And opens your soul to become the
recipient of what He knows.
To clearly observe what He loves and what He hates,
And know for certain what He
will and will not tolerate.

You see through the eyes of His Word.
And understand His disciplines.
Your life is healthy, your soul wealthy,
You are overshadowed by the King of Kings.

But, there lies one who desires
the moisture in your soil.
And seeks to shrivel up the seed
that lives within you.
Your eye contact with God is despised.
Because you are uncontrollable
when you are eye to eye.

Forgiveness

Prelude

Life presents a variety of situations and circumstances. Some you invite in, while others are set in your lap whether you want them or not. What do you do with the things you do not want? How do you handle the things you did not ask for? What do you do with hurt, pain, and affliction? There was a time in my life when I was consumed with contemplation of how to afflict the one or ones who had injured me. I came to realize the only one I was damaging was me. Forgiveness was not a consideration because I could not see beyond the insult and injury. It was as if I was living in a capsulated moment, frozen in the occurrence and bound by self.

When God began to deal with me about forgiveness, I did not think it was possible. How could you relinquish all of the hurt and let the person or people go free? I did not understand and I did not comprehend forgiveness. God explained forgiveness to me in a way which allowed my mortal mind to grasp. "Forgiveness is not necessarily for the other person; it is for you. It sets you free! You are free to live, laugh, and love. You are freed from bondage, hurt, pain, and the tragic anguish that so cripples you. You lose the attachments of the offenses and set yourself as well as the offender free. You are free to move through life without restraints on your mind, heart and life. Forgiveness liberates you."

The instant I finally surrendered to God's instruction, I physically felt something leave from my body. I cannot adequately explain what it was; however, it was as though a heaviness or weight was lifted. When I felt that release, I said, "Oh God, had I known that I could be free from all of this, I would have forgiven long ago. Please do not ever allow me to become unforgiving again."

I love feeling the deliverance, freedom, and liberty forgiveness brings. Life introduces an array of challenges in which some situations are easier to forgive than others. Whatever the matter, forgive. If at all possible, forgive quickly. Your life depends on it. If it is taking more than a few moments, lay yourself before God so that He can help you get rid of the poison. You do not want to kill yourself with the toxic bitterness an unforgiving heart produces. Besides, it is not God's desire for you to be bound but to always be free. Forgive!

I am a wounded vessel.
The broken pieces lay on the inside.
I am shattered like glass.
With no more tears to cry,
I think I can die.

How do I rise from here?
How do I stand up?
My heart is faint,
And my strength is weak.
How can I collect the pieces?

"Forgive," I heard Him say.
"Forgive them!"
"I don't want to forgive!"
Cried the rebel in me.
"I am broken and hurting."

"Forgive," I heard Him say.
"Forgive them!
Forgiveness is for your sake.
Release them and set yourself free.
Forgive them and release your heart to Me."

So I gave God everything.
I lifted my hands and surrendered it all to Him.
The shackles broke and the weight lifted.
No longer bound in the prison of my pain,
God wiped it away like fresh rain.

The wounded vessel is now healed.
He said, "This is how you are to live."
The pieces that were shattered like glass,
The finger of God healed all the cracks.
Now I live, now I breathe; now I love freely.

Persuasions

Prelude

It is imperative that you pay close attention to the people who have your ear. These are the people closest to you; the people who have the ability to persuade your decisions. It matters not whether they are your family, friends, or coworkers. You are responsible to always guard your mind as well as your heart. You must be careful to hear the heart of the one speaking to you. Are they giving you sound instruction or speaking words that will cause your destruction? Do their words align with truth, or will they take you off course and carry your feet somewhere God has not ordained you to go? Be careful of who you allow to influence your decisions. Choices, whether good or bad, affect your life forever! Be careful of who you allow to *whisper* in your inner ear.

Who has your ear?
Who has the power to persuade you
in one direction or another?
Who do you listen to?
Whose words in secret or openly do you consider,
When you make decisions?
To whom have you submitted your trust?
To whom do you offer your mind?

Who has the power to sway you?
By simply speaking into your ear?
Who carries the ability to influence your decisions?

With the one who is whispering?
Can you hear the conviction to do right?
Or can you perceive the sound of wrong?
Is it for your benefit?
Or is it for their covert gain?
You must be very careful,
With whom you allow to have access into your mind.
You must weigh their words,
Because their words can build you or kill you.

Out of the abundance of the heart, the mouth tells.
Be very careful to discern the heart of the speaker,
Simply by listening to what is flowing from their lips.
Is your best interest sincerely held
within the contents of their heart?
However, if you really desire an accurate influence,
A proper Friend you can always trust.
Recognize God in all your ways,
And He will surely direct your paths.

Counsel

Prelude

Life is extremely fast-paced in the era in which we live. We live in a microwave society and do not have the patience or tolerance for much of anything. We want what we want, and we want it now! We are spoiled. Yes, we are. Although things have changed and technology has tremendously advanced and catapulted us into the extreme speed lane on the highway of life, God has not changed! We are driven to do things quickly because time is of the essence.

I agree. Time is of the essence. It is our most valuable asset and should not be wasted. Some say time is money. I say time is life. Manage it wisely. We are so rushed that we do not reserve or set time aside for God. He has to literally interrupt our thoughts and lives to get our attention. Stop, pray and listen. He is attempting to invest in our daily lives so we can be blessed. We cannot be so hurried that we fail to acknowledge Him and the instruction and direction He wants to impart in us. We must slow down and take the time to hear what God has to say. It could save your life! This is a lesson learned. Had I truly considered my time with God, it would not have been necessary for Him to utter the words, "Slow down and pay attention."

Pay attention to My voice.
I'm trying to get your attention.
You need to hear Me.
There are things I need you to see.
There are things that I need you to recognize.

Slow down, you are moving too fast.
You are passing too quickly,
By the thing I need you to take notice of.
Pay attention to Me.
Pay attention to what I am attempting to teach you.

Pay attention to what you see.
Pay close attention to what you do not or cannot see.
Be keen and sharp in the Spirit.
I am preparing you for something great.

Be careful to not get caught in distractions,
For they are diversions and tactics
that are not from Me,
But methods to distract you from
Me and your purpose.
Be careful to obey My Word.

Be careful!

He Is All I Have

Prelude

Anytime I meditate on God and trace my life, my mind is flooded with the wonders of who He is, what He has done, how He has carried, lifted, watched over, protected, and blessed me. He was and is always where I am. I belong to Him and He belongs to me. He is all that I have in this life and beyond. What an everlasting companion. I love Him so much!

Jesus is all I have.
When I look through my life,
I cannot find one who cares for me more than He.

At times I have cried inside,
And He has dried my naked eyes;
And when I have been down and
low, He has uplifted my head.

He considers me,
And hears me when I call out to Him.
He responds to me.

He is always here,
Never far away,
Within a breath's reach.

He beckons me to come,
That I may rest in Him.
He hands out no more than what I can contain.

He sits on His throne,
And with His compassionate love for me,
He calculates my path.

He desires that I am free,
To live here in abundance.
He testifies of His goodness and kindness.

He is more than remarkable,
Always willing,
Desperately wanting to attend to my every need.

For He is God!
Forever desiring my submission,
That I may know who He is to
me and who I am in Him.

I am important to God.
I am significant!
To Him alone I belong, and He is all I have.

Blown Away

Prelude

When I attempt to figure God out, I am lost in my own thoughts. It is like a cork bobbing in the middle of the ocean. I am too small and He is too grand. It is not that God has not taught me who He is. He has. It is in the teaching that I have realized there is so much more to learn. It keeps me humble because I am aware that what I have come to know is like me spitting in the sea. When I make the comparison of what I have learned to what I do not know, I am overwhelmed. It drives me to seek Him more, to know Him more and find Him. Not that He is lost or hiding; He is so infinite I must search Him out. God is high, low, wide, and very, very deep. I understand that I am still just scraping the surface of my discoveries of Him.

The thought keeps circling in my mind,
But I cannot apprehend it.
The purity of God's love.
I am lost in my thoughts,
Attempting to discern the heart of God.
It is too wonderful,
Too inconceivable,
The breadth, the height, the length,
and depth of God's love.

I am humbled to my knees,
And in His presence I lay prostrate.

In spite of what I am not,
He remains relentless.
His love is in constant pursuit of me,
To reveal to me His true identity.
I am unfamiliar with this magnitude of passion.
It frightens me.
What if I awake to find it is not?
How shall I continue,
Now that I have tasted such a surpassing love?
Even in this, He has assured me,
He will never leave me nor forsake me,
And the rhythm of the beat of
my heart is made steady.

I can only imagine,
Standing before Him, feeling His
breath touch my face,
With my eternity wrapped in the surety of His arms.
Oh how I long to grasp the reality of His wonder!
Yet He is so beyond my realm of imagination,
And any means by which I have
understood anything.
God is just too magnificent!
His love is more than what my
humanity can comprehend.

The thought continues to circle in my mind,
The purity of God's love for me.
It is too wonderful!
And I must confess,
I have yet to comprehend it!

Thoughts

Prelude

I am familiar with molestation of the mind. Let me share this with you. As you know, all thoughts are not your own. You know this, right? You have three major influences that affect how you think. Your thoughts, God's influence by the Holy Spirit, and the devil pitching an idea that is contrary to the will of God. You're probably asking, "What about friends, family and foes?" They are the minor three. The majors are the ones I want you to consider, so read this carefully. Have you ever been going about your day when a thought came into your mind, and you asked yourself, "Where did that come from?" You were not thinking about the matter that entered your mind but knew it was against the will or Word of God.

That is how the enemy manipulates you. He is constantly toying with your mind, distracting you in order to fracture your thoughts to insert and process his own. All he desires is for you to give him access to a very small opening. He will then attempt to insert vain imaginations that are against the information of God. He will pitch a thought over and over again until you take hold of the idea as if it were your own. So now you consider this newly implanted notion and contemplate the thought your mind has swallowed up. You own it now, it belongs to you, and you allow its digestion to take place and enter into your heart. You now not only consider the idea, you have developed an illegal passion to pursue it. Your feet carry your whole body away in deception because you embraced a thought that was not yours or God's. It was the devil's! Guard your heart and your mind. The devil is out to distract and molest your mind against the Word of God concerning your life. If you are not careful to cast down vain thoughts immediately when they occur, he will trick you into carrying out offenses against your own life. Remember the minor three, friend, family and foe? The devil can use their voices to molest your mind as well.

Be conscious of your thoughts.
The enemy is very clever,
To introduce seducing thoughts into your mind,
That you did not initiate.
Have you ever been going through your day,
And a thought entered your mind,
That was so contrary to what your
thoughts were at that time?
And you questioned yourself…
Where did that come from?
You knew that it was not a God thought.

The devil likes to molest your mind.
He enjoys trying to break into your
thoughts to insert his own,
Persuading you to acknowledge and consider
the thought he attempts to plant,
Over and over, again and again.

Now his thought become your thought,
And you cannot distinguish the difference,
Because you have embraced the
devil's thought as your own.
And now you consider it over and over,
Thinking about it constantly,
So much so that it has now fallen into your heart,
And becomes your heart's illegal desire to pursue.

Now you find your feet are carrying your whole body,
Somewhere God never intended for you to go.
You find yourself desiring what you know is sin,
And then find yourself participating
in the acts of them.
You have been psychologically molested by the devil,
And what entered your mind has
infected your passions.
Now seduced and entangled,
You find yourself trapped, seeking,
but finding no way out.
You cannot understand how you
ended up where you are.
Saying to yourself, "I knew better than to do this!"
Remember what the Word of God says …

The weapons of our warfare are not fleshly,
But powerful in God for casting down strongholds,
Casting down opinions,
And every elevated thing that exalts itself,
Against the information of God,
Bringing every thought into confinement,
Unto the obedience of Christ.

Be careful what you entertain in your mind.
It will make your feet go where God never intended.

Authenticity

Preface

Always be true to yourself. You will meet people in your life who will attempt to critique you into becoming who they think you should be. The truth be told, they have yet to come into the knowledge of who they are themselves. Consider this, if the correction will benefit, edify, or help you become a better human being, be grateful that someone cares enough to say anything. If it is to form you into their design; do not let them do it. You will be lost for years trying to figure out who you are and possibly die never discovering the truth. God created you and me as original masterpieces.

I can remember family, strangers and friends suggesting how I should or should not be. Some was beneficial and some needed to be trashed. I tend to be a very truthful person. It has been my experience that most people do not want the truth, cannot receive the truth, or want you to sugarcoat it in some way. I have been told that I am too direct. Some people assess my directness as being harsh. My intention was not to be harsh but to be honest. I did evaluate myself, but I did not withdraw from being truthful or honest. I do not know how, nor do I desire to learn any technique in being less than truthful with another person. I view that as being deceptive. God is still developing patience and grace in me. He has not completed me yet. I am still growing and learning how to walk in His ways. With that said, I still cannot allow myself to be less than truthful. I have; however, begun making a conscious effort to convey truths in a manner that is easily received. In all honesty, I am still working on it! That bit of constructive criticism I received as being profitable.

We are to be honest and truthful and deal with people fairly; this is Scripture. I do not know your story, but mine deals with being an honest and truthful person. This is just one scenario out of many. The important thing is to be true to who God created you to be. You were made in His image to be the reflection of who He is. You might have to sand down the rough edges, but don't lose the core of the God-created person. You will be different. You will stand apart and sometimes alone. I guarantee, you will be viewed as a peculiar person because you will not fit into the categories of other people. You will find comfort in the category God created you to be in. Do not spend your time trying to be the copycat of another person. Be authentic. Be original. No one can be you better than the you God created.

God created you like no other;
You are not a duplicate!
You are the original.
You are the authentic masterpiece.
You are created in His image by His hands.

Be aligned with your true self,
Not a copycat of someone else.
It is easy to discern the authentic:
You have never seen anyone like them before.
They are a peculiar people.
It is something about them,
That sets them apart from the rest.
If you are not careful,
You will mimic what you see.
You must discover your own originality.
You must possess your own identity.
There is not a match for your peculiar DNA.
There is no two of you.
That is how creatively distinguished you are by God.
So be the God-created person that you are.
The one who has visions and dreams, dreams.
The vision and dreams God ignited within you.
The true essence of who you are.
The person you are destined to be.
Believe you can, and you will.
And never lose the faith!
God created you an authentic masterpiece.
He never intended for you to be
a copycat of an original.

Save the World

Prelude

This is a really interesting song because I was actually lying in bed trying to sleep when I heard it. I think it is rather immediate. In other words, it has implications. God is coming after you, me and everybody else, ready or not. As a believer, it is imperative that you and I make a conscious effort to tell the world who God is. This song conveys the responsibility of a person of faith to tell the world about the One who created it and all that it contains. As a believer you are a "world changer." You were born to change the world by witnessing to one created being at a time. You are to articulate the love of God in whatever form God desires.

You go through your day,
Not thinking what may come your way.
People watch what you do,
What you say.
You've got to live by the Word,
Not just saying what you've heard.
Father wants us to do His will.
Save the world.
Change the world.

Jesus ran His race.
He beat the enemy to his face.
He set an example by which we are to live by.
He held on to the faith.
Father's love abounded in grace.
He did what the Father wanted Him to do.
Save the world.
Change the world.

"Just let them know," He said.
"I'm here and I love them so.
Soon I'll be back, and you must be ready.
The time is close at hand.
Your soul I will demand,
And every work of your hand."
Save the world.
Change the world.

"Read the writings in the sky.
They will tell you why.
Earthquakes are in many places.
Men cry out peace.
All around there is war.
Know that I am at your door."
Save the world.
Change the world.

Joy

Prelude

I am sure that we all have had seasons in our lives, which were neither appealing nor attractive to us. We have had times when our hearts beat faintly and sorrow robbed us of our joy. When the morning came, it was no sweeter than the day before we laid our heads upon our pillows. During such a season, this hymn was birthed. Remarkably, it was in this season and in this state of sadness that God taught me how to pray and worship regardless of how I felt.

I remember when God spoke to me and said, "Prayer is not based on how you feel. Regardless of what you feel and what you are going through, I am still God and worthy to be praised." Sorrow has the ability to paralyze you. If you are not careful, you will find yourself disconnected from the only One who is more than able and willing to help you: God. Once I heard God speak those words in my spirit, I had to press my way into the throne room and lay myself at His feet. There at His feet, when I began to declare His goodness, mercy, faithfulness, loving kindness, greatness, and virtue, God touched me and strengthened my spirit. It ignited the beginning of the return of my joy.

God is God. He is more than able to do exceedingly great things on your behalf. This is His Word. In spite of current happenings, if you would just pray, worship and believe, God can heal your soul and restore your life.

I woke up this morning, feeling down.
I prayed and asked the Lord, "Please turn it around.
You said, "Joy comes in the morning,"
So "Where then, Lord, is my smile?"

I prayed out and called out your name,
"Lord, deliver me from this pain.
I'm hurt and I need your touch right now,
On my knees to you I pray and do bow."
You said, "Joy comes in the morning."
Well then, "Where, Dear Lord, is my smile?"

I lifted up my hands and praised your name,
"Bless you, Jesus"; your Spirit came!
It fell upon me and wrapped me round and round,
And on my face my smile I found.
You said, "Joy comes in the morning,"
And here, "Oh God is my smile."

You know, I have to praise your name,
Regardless of the circumstances,
regardless of the pain,
So I lift my voice and bless you anyway.
You always comfort me,
And stand me to my feet,
Pour strength deep inside of me.

Joy comes in the morning!
And thank You, Father God,
For my smile.
Thank You, Lord,
For my smile.

Dance with Me

Prelude

As I was sitting on my bedroom floor, as I often do and talk with God, I heard myself say, "God, I want to dance with You." As soon as I heard it, I began to apologize to God for saying what I had heard myself say. I had not considered or thought about dancing with God. As soon as I heard those words, I believed I was out of line.

I said to the Lord, "I'm sorry. You are not so common that I should petition You as a simple man." It interrupted my prayer! I began to question myself. Why did I say that? Where did that come from? I never had the idea, nor had I ever thought or even considered dancing with God. I was disturbed! The following day, as I worshipped and prayed the same words came from my mouth. I apologized again to the Lord and wondered why I continued to utter these words. A couple of days passed and I had just come out of prayer and was running out of the house. Angella, a friend of mine, was waiting in her car for me. As I left the house to get into her car, I began hearing this song in my spirit. I then understood that it was not my request to dance with God, but it was God's desire to dance with me! I was wowed!

I want you to move to the rhythm
of the beat of My heart,
Flow with Me to finish what I began to start.
I want to take you by the hand,
Lead you by My command,
Can I have this dance with you?

I don't want to dance with you for a moment,
And I don't want to dance with you for an hour.
I want to dance in your morning light,
Through your afternoon;
I want to dance into eternity with you!

Like a vapor that blows in the wind,
It moves and it flows,
Wherever the breath of wind blows it.
It has no reserve; there's no resistance.
That's how I want you to be, totally free.

Can I have this dance, My child?
You see, I want the dance!
Can I have this dance with you?

False Reality

Preface

How many of us live under the cloud of fear? I am not referring to a real threat that causes you to be afraid of someone or something. I am talking about believing what is not truth. Embracing what does not exist. Let me give you an example. The first time in my life that I felt absolutely elated and happy to the fullest extent, something happened! In the midst of that feeling, suddenly I became conscious of what I was feeling and became fearful. Fear seized that elated feeling and deflated that moment. In the midst of that particular moment, I thought, *This is so wonderful; it cannot last.* There was a fear that the feeling would not last because something devastating would happen to take it away. From that day forward, for many years, every time I felt exhilarated a dreadful thought passed through my mind. As time went on I became less excited about life's possibilities because I believed happiness could not last. Something tragic was bound to happen to wipe it all away. Needless to say, it was a false reality. It wasn't real. It wasn't even truth.

When God delivered me from that mindset, it was like pulling layers of fear off my mind. Literally! Envision the sky being covered by rags, and the rags being pulled off one at a time until the entire spectrum of the sky was clear. That is what I experienced when God delivered me. I had reached a certain level of joy. There was a ceiling in my mind that I could not penetrate. Joy, excitement, laughter and elation were out of my reach due to a perpetual thought of fleeting happiness. I had allowed this dread to attach itself to my mind. I understood it was imagined, but I could not shake it. It tripped me up for years. God; who is just and faithful summoned His Word to minister to me. Through the Word, I was reminded that this is not how He ordained me to live my life. The Word loosened shackles and broke bondages that I had lived with for years. I no longer feared happiness. I was free! It is so wonderful to be free and to know, "Yes, God does want me to be happy!"

The Word of God teaches us that we are not given the spirit of fear but of power, love, and a sound mind. The devil comes to kill, steal and destroy. He loves to toy with your mind and seduce you into believing what is not truth. It is in your mind where you will fight the greatest battles of your life. If you are dealing with false realities, lay yourself before God and ask Him to deliver you from that spirit. He can set you free to live in the fullness of what He has declared over your life. It is not the will of God for you to be subdued by falsities or fears. It is the *will* of God that your joy be full!

What has seized your members?
What has paralyzed you?
That you will not live or be,
The one I created?

Fear has captured you!
Like one caught in a trap,
But there is no trap to be caught in.
Who has tricked you to believe what is not?

Your heart beats viciously,
At the fear that has spooked you.
But where is the truth for your reason?
Where is the evidence for your torment?

Who has fooled you?
For it is written,
God has not given a spirit of fear,
But of power, love, and a sound mind.

Fear is a non-existent reality.
Free your mind from that which is not.
Succumb to it no more.
For you are free in God to live life abundantly.

All of Me

Preface

Early one morning, as I sat at my kitchen table enjoying the presence of the Lord, I heard this hymn. The Lord explained to me with lyrics, melody, and rhymes, my need for Him in every situation in my life. He revealed to me where I fell short and why I was not making the mark. I thought this was so beautiful because it caused me to assess myself. God is so faithful. He will never leave you where you are; rather, He will expose you to yourself so that you can identify where you are in Him and where growth is needed. He desires that you receive the best He has to offer. He can then acquire and delight in the gifts He has so graciously endowed.

I want you to take all of Me.
You can't receive just part of Me!
You want to accept some of Me;
The rest you want to leave.
You need all of Me.

You read My Word,
You say you believe in what you have heard,
But when troubles come you want to run,
Say it's too hard so you disregard,
You need all of Me.

You want a part-time love,
Forgetting that I am a full-time God,
I give all of Myself.
How could you want something else?
You just need Me.

You want to do it your way.
How can you live in the fullness of what I say,
Or what I've called you to be?
Truly, free indeed,
It takes every bit, every part, all of Me.

How can you posses what I have?
Keep it in the cleft of your small human hand,
Guard it in your heart.
I'm telling you it's not just part,
You need all of Me.

All of Me.
How can you live outside of that reality?
I am your source for all things,
Into existence I bring.
Do you believe Me?

One on One

Prelude

I remember when I heard the Lord speak to my heart about praying at a specific time. I recall thinking that this particular time would interrupt the middle of my day. I asked the Lord, "What do You want me to pray about? I pray in the morning and I pray at night. What else do You want me to talk to You about?" I did not hear Him respond to me, so at the designated time, I obeyed God.

On the first day of my new journey, I stood before the Lord and asked, "What should I pray?" I heard the Lord tell me to worship. I asked, "How?" I understood worship as the way you live your surrendered life unto God; your obedience! This was different! This was something I had never done before. He began to teach me how to glorify, adore and magnify Him. It was not a time set aside to ask Him for anything. It was simply a time between He and I. It was a time specifically set aside to declare how wonderful and awesome He is. God *is* incredible and continues to amaze me. It was from this heart-to-heart relationship that He began to speak to me in hymns, songs, poems, writings and revelation of His Word. It was the beginning of this book that you are now holding and reading in your hand.

Your day cannot be so filled with life,
That you spend no time with God.
Your days cannot be so busy,
That you do not acknowledge Him.
You must carve time from out of your day,
That is just for Him alone.
There must be some one-on-one time with God.
Time just between the two of you,
Time spent building intimacy and
relationship between you.

This is time to bless Him for His faithfulness,
Worship Him for who He is.
Praise Him for His wondrous works,
Thank Him for His goodness and kindness.
Bask in His presence, asking for nothing;
Listen to understand the beat of His heart,
Hear His secrets spoken into your ear.
Stand still in the company of the King,
And be swept away by His awesome presence.

God is not so busy with the events of the day,
That He does not acknowledge you,
Or so filled with the current issues,
That He has no desire to spend time with you.
He desires your one-on-one with Him.
You must seize the time!
And make room for relationship with God.

Intercourse

Prelude

The word *intercourse* is an interesting word because most people affix it with a sexual connotation. It defines more than sexual acts. When we think about intercourse in relation to God, it is simply an exchange between God and man. It is the interchange of our thoughts exchanged for His thoughts, our will exchanged for His will, and our ways exchanged for His ways. We surrender and submit our lives to God in exchange to live the life of Christ. Intercourse is the total submission to God through Christ Jesus. It is surrendering all that you are for all that He is. Intercourse is the ultimate exchange of your mind, will, and emotions for the mind, will and passions of Christ. We who are transformed are to occupy until He comes. In order to be like Him, we must first have intercourse with Him.

There is an exchange between God and man.
An exchange from heaven to the earth.
An exchange from the supernatural to the natural.
An exchange from the spirit to the tangible.
An exchange from God.

God trades your heart for His heart.
Your mind for His mind.
He exchanges your thoughts for His thoughts.
And your will for His.
Your passions for His passions.
Your character for His character.

Surprisingly you find yourself looking
through the eyes of God.
Viewing things considerably different,
With drastic changes to your perception,
Intercourse begins to take place.
You begin to transform,
Shedding old ways and pulling down mindsets.

This is not just any transformation;
This is an eternal exchange of who you are,
For who God is.
And you must surrender to intercourse with God,
And submit yourself to Him.

Be transformed by His Spirit,
Into the full stature of who you are in His will.
And when intercourse has its way,
Then, you will see life through the lenses of God,
And understand His intentions
for you, as well as man.

Praying at Attention

Prelude

God has instructed us to come boldly before Him and make our requests known. We are to come into His courts with thanksgiving and praise. I have to admit that I became a slouch with regard to attentiveness in prayer. The writing that follows makes this apparent. I would not otherwise have been so corrected. Sometimes we think we are doing the right thing but fail to recognize we have carried it out the wrong way.

When we pray, there are instances when we must fight our mind to bring our thoughts under control. I have personally experienced going before the Lord in prayer with an uncontrollable mind. This is how the Lord addressed my nomadic mind. I am so glad God does not just toss us to the side. I am grateful that He knows I am in desperate, desperate need of Him. When we disappoint Him, He has unlimited generosity, mercy and grace. He desires that you and I return to His fountain daily to be refilled.

When you come before Me, the Lord of Hosts, into my holy chamber to visit Me in prayer, think upon these things and consider this; you visited a good friend's house. When you arrived, your friend was excited to see you and allowed you to enter. Your friend sat in your presence and began to commune with you. You were so excited because the relationship is one that you honor and greatly treasure. Yet, the mind of your friend wandered to unseen internal distractions. You relentlessly attempted to communicate; however, your friend's attention became divided. You realized you were no longer being acknowledged. Your friend's mind had drifted elsewhere and was completely disengaged as though you were no longer present. You knew your friend would not receive the importance or value of what you needed to speak into his life. Your friend left your presence empty and did not receive what was most significant and necessary.

When you come before Me to pray, bring your thoughts into subjection. Do not drift! Pray at attention! I have something extremely significant to speak into your life that you need to hear every day. How would you feel if you came before Me and My thoughts drifted elsewhere? You come to pray, and I do not pay attention. I disregard your presence as though you were not there because I am distracted! This is not a testimony of Myself! You have My undivided attention. Give me yours when you pray.

The Fight

Prelude

I love using vibrant colors in my house, especially on my walls. One day, I was painting my nook in my kitchen in hues of purple and gold with a hint of red. Anyway, I was on the ladder with roller in hand, and as I was painting the wall, the thought of a particular brother in the ministry named Marvin came to mind. I could see him clearly. As I thought of him, an overwhelming sense of hopelessness and fatigue came upon me. It was as though I felt what he felt—worn out and tired! What I experienced was translated into a hymn. This hymn was for him. When I saw him at church, I told him what had occurred while painting my wall. I sang to him what the Lord had given me. He looked in my eyes and said, "Thank you sis. I needed that."

God is always thinking about you and me. When no one else sees what you are going through, God is taking notice! When your journey has become so strained and overwhelming that you cannot hear God or the predicaments of life have smothered the sound of His voice; God will send a brother, sister, preacher, or prophet to give you a word. This word will realign you back into position and cause you to remember who He is and recall the promises He has made to you. God will revive your soul. If you diligently seek Him, He will never leave you where you are. He will;

however, leave you with a testimony of His greatness, goodness, and of how He brought you out.

There's no time for hanging your head down low.
There's no time for feeling sad.
There's no time for giving up on God's Word,
For the battle is heated now,
And there's no time to throw in the towel.

There's no time for your heart to give in.
There's no time to debate what you've
heard over and over again.
It seems like it's been so long.
You've got to keep pressing on!
For the battle is heated now,
And there is no time to throw in the towel.

For the promise is coming to find you.
Will you be found doing what the
Lord has instructed you to do?
Will the Word find a place,
Where it can remain,
To perform the will of the Lord?

The battle is heated now,
And there's no time to throw in the towel.

Lord Hear Me

Prelude

Have you ever been in a situation or in the midst of a circumstance in which you just did not know what to do? I have on more than one occasion! The Word of God teaches us to acknowledge God in all our ways and He will direct our paths. Even in the midst of confusion, the Word can and will settle your mind if you submit and surrender to its instruction. God is faithful to fulfill His Word and do as He said, if you do as He asks. Do not be anxious, but with prayer and supplication make your request known before the Lord. Wait on Him, and He will give you His wisdom to make the right decisions.

Lord, I need You to listen to my cries.
I need You to hear the concerns in my life.
You are the only One who has the
power to make change.
You are the only One who understands my pain.

There are so many questions that I have.
I find no answers as I search within myself.
I need to hear Your counsel,
Speak to me clear.
I need to understand.
Help me to know Your will.

This place in my life seems so hard.
I don't know what I should do, Lord!
So Father, here I am.
I turn to You for the answers that I seek.
Show me Your way.
You are the lamp under my feet.

Lord, You are the way, the truth; You are my life!
Where else can I go?
Who else can I go to?
Not only do You have the answer,
But You are the answer,
To the sum of my life.

Lord, I need You to listen to my cries.
I need You to hear the concerns in my life.
You are the only One who has the
power to make change.
You are the only One who understands my pain.

Much

Prelude

Who is like God? There is no one like Him! When I think, consider, and meditate on who He is, I get lost in His grandeur. When I consider creation and ponder the thought of the wonder of it all, I am in awe. When I look at a sunrise and behold the beauty of a sunset, I am bewildered. Who can explain it? Who can explain what God has done? Who is capable of articulating it for me?

I look at the stars draped across the heavens as they spread out above me; it is so incredible. I look at myself and I am reminded of all people that God created in His image. I think about how gracious, kind and loving He is to me and soon find myself on my knees as His presence covers me and His hand touches me. I come to Him again and again to comprehend who He is. I cannot grasp Him all in one setting. I return over and over again and again. I am so grateful that He would share Himself with me.

When I consider the vastness of You,
I cannot lie to myself and say that I understand.
For You are too much for me to comprehend,
too much for me to grasp.

You are more than my mind can
process in a single setting.
I must visit You over and over, again and again.
My mind cannot contain You!
Yet I know You are!
I *know* You are real.

Sometimes I am terrified of Your reality
and the tangibility of Your presence.
I am in awe of You!
The more I learn, the less I know.
I have discovered through Your revelation
of who You are I know nothing.
It is not that I have not learned of You.
It is just that the more I learn, the more I realize
I have just caught a glimpse of who You are,
As though I had blinked my eye.

There is an overwhelming measure of so
much more that I must seek to capture.
In this truth I rest in You, trusting You,
for I see that You are more than I.
So supreme and excellent!
So majestic and wonderful!
Full of power and authority!
You are magnified in my life!

Who is like You? Who?
There is none!
There is no one to compare You
with or compare You to.
To even suggest that there is, or give thought
to the possibility, is simply ludicrous.

To You be all honor and glory
forever and ever, Father!
Be glorified in the heavens and in the earth!
And hide me in Thyself always.

Extra

Prelude

There is so much deception in life. It is introduced in a variety of ways. If you do not know what the truth is, how do you identify deception? Everybody seems to have an opinion of how someone should perform in life. Those opinions are usually regulated by how one feels, how they view a situation or the opinion is extracted from a life experience. Just because you feel something does not make it truth. Just because you believe something does not make it the truth either. There is a difference between what is *true* and what the *truth* is. Truth is pure, whole, the absence of everything that is lie. There are things that are true, but they are not necessarily the truth. God is true and truth! You must know what God said and what God did not say. When a conversation with anyone introduces a misrepresentation of the truth of God, you cannot allow the words spoken in that conversation to cause you to go against or disagree with the words of God.

Let's step into the Garden of Eden for a moment. When Eve was deceived she was not deceived by the truth, she was deceived by the misrepresentation of the truth. The devil or serpent toyed with her mind by playing with God's words. The devil knew what God had commanded Adam and Eve, but he did not respect the commandment. The serpent says to Eve, "Did God really say, you are not to eat from any tree in the garden?" Here he pricks her mind by seducing her with a question contrary to the information she already knew was true and truth from God. Her response to the serpent was exactly what God had said. "We may eat from the fruit of the trees of the garden, but from the fruit of the tree in the middle of the garden, God said, 'You are neither to eat from it nor touch it, or you will die.'" The serpent releases a direct assault against the truth God spoke with a bold and deadly lie. "It is *not* true that you will surely die; God knows on the day you eat from it, your eyes will be opened and you will be like God, knowing good and evil." Now we have the fall. Eve traded what God said for what the serpent said. She believed the serpent instead of God. She traded the truth for a lie and they died, as God had said. His word is true and the truth.

There are many distractions, illusions, persuasions, and deceptions that will trip your feet and cause you to stumble and fall away from God. Be careful what you watch and be careful whom you allow access to your ear gate. Guard your mind and seek diligently to understand the difference between the truth and a lie. Live.

There is truth and there is a lie.
Can man discern between the two?
Can one discern good or evil?
What a man thinks is true does not make it truth.

And one's perception of truth
does not make it a reality.
It is only one's perception or
perceived truth, not the truth!
Which if not careful leads to self deception,
And causes one to lie in the bed
of self-deceit, peacefully,
Living in a lie and believing it to be true.
Only God can separate the two,
That you may know the difference,
And without Him, you know no truth,
For He alone is the way, the truth, and the life.

You hear men say, "If it feels good, do it."
What feels good to you will kill you!
In more ways than one.
Can you number them?
The emotions of men are not always accurate.
Did you not know that the heart
is most deceitfully wicked?
And the wickedness of your own heart,
Will cause your feet to carry you,
To places God never intended for you to go.
It takes God to settle your emotions and feelings,
To cause you to not act out illegal passions,
But rather, instruct you by the wisdom
He places in your mind,
Wisdom that is only given upon request.

This is just extra.
You can take it or leave it!
You can embrace it or reject it.
It's up to you.

Because the truth is still the truth.
And a lie is still a lie.
And when it is all said and done,
You must still choose.
You can choose the truth, or you can choose a lie.
Just remember, only God can separate the two,
That you may know the difference.
And without Him, you know no truth,
For He alone is the way, the truth, and the life.

Sons of Men

Prelude

I have seen people suffer through so much. Some people endure much more than others and some less than most. It seems that no matter who you talk to, someone is going through something, or they have come out of something. I am no exception. My experience with God has taught me that He is always available. If I open my mouth and call on Him, He is here ! He is not just God up in the big sky! He is God who is right here for me. He is here for you as well. He is so close; right on the tip of your tongue. If you would just call on His name—Jesus! He will answer.

I see the sons of men,
Weighed down, down low,
No idea where to go.
No idea what to do.
Prayer would give them an answer.
But in the midst of their troubles,
They cannot identify its need.
The need for You to show them their way,
A path laid by Your wisdom,
To not stumble through their day.

Men are dying;
The hearts of men are crying.
They commit spiritual suicide.
Not knowing You are here,

Blinded to the truth that You care.
They need to know,
You love them the most,
And their lives fit in the palm of Your hand.
But the sons of men don't understand.
Because they know not of You.

Lord, when we see the sons of men,
Your dearly beloved children,
Help us to intercede,
And pray with sincere fervor for their need.
You are the One and only true hope.
The only One who can strengthen men to cope.
Help them to take You by Your hand.
Lead them by Your wisdom and instruction.
Bless men that they may truly know,
That You deeply love them so.

Confidence

Prelude

I am sure there has been an occasion in your life when it appeared everything was caving in around you. The very ground you were standing on felt absent of substance. It possibly appeared as though your situations and circumstances were testifying against what you believed. The visible, tangible aspects of life began to break down the invisible, infallible truths. You found it difficult to hold on to your faith. Nevertheless, the faithfulness of God showed up. He helped you remember who He is and what He has already done on your behalf. He reassured you that He is with you always, even in the most trying situations. He reignites your faith and stirs your confidence in who He said He is. He comforts you to again lie in the lap of His truth, regardless of the set of issues that you face. He settles your spirit by reminding you of His wonder and glorious splendor. There is nothing that is too great or impossible for God. Trials come to make you strong. Rejoice, for when they are over; they leave you stronger and wiser than you previously were.

Why has your face fallen?
Why are you so dismayed and discontented?
Have you so soon forgotten your
Lord God whom you serve?

Have you forgotten all the wonders and
miracles I have performed for you?

I, God, brought you through the storm once!
Will I not do it again?
Who and what has robbed you of your faith?
Child of the living and most High God,
The devil is a liar!

For I have committed Myself to see you
succeed through every tribulation,
Through every storm, through every trial,
Circumstance and situation that
could ever exist in your life.
I understand you!
Have I not been touched with like things?

Therefore, commit yourself to Me!
Cleave to Me!
Stay with Me in My Word and in My Will,
Know that I am the Lord thy God,
who stands with you!
Be confident and fully persuaded in whom you serve!

A Time for Love

Prelude

It never ceases to amaze me how God can suddenly put a song in my heart. I marvel how He causes me to scribe and how the word reveals itself as ink flows from pen to paper. I wrote this poem one evening at work. It was a quiet evening, and most of the staff had gone home. The ones who remained had pretty much completed their tasks for the evening, making it quiet and still. As I was sitting at my desk waiting for my shift to end, these particular words ran through my mind. I looked for a piece of paper to write the words down. When I finished, I read what I had written and thought, *Wow, this is beautiful!* He has given me an expected life. I can anticipate a divine course set by God. I really am grateful for God's plan for my life.

This is the heart of God for His people. It is for you and me and the rest of the human population. Regardless if people do not recognize, acknowledge or see that you are significant, God does! You are of great value to Him. God has something incredible in store for your life. Oh yes, He does! You and I are shrouded in the divine plan God has purposed for us. He has assembled a life filled with extraordinary expectations. God is so generous with His love.

When everyone passed you by,
And no one acknowledged you,
Or had compassion on you,
And you were looked upon as though
you had nothing to offer,
You began to believe you were nothing
because you were treated as such.
And with all that is within the
earth, you were so alone.

But when I, God, passed by you and saw you,
I looked at you and had pity on you.
And I declared within Myself,
It is "A Time for Love."

And I, Love, stretched out My
arms open wide and said,
"Come ... for I have declared you to be
more than what you have believed.
For I know the thoughts that I think toward you,
Thoughts of peace and not of evil, to
give you an end with expectations.

For I am the mender of the lonely
and brokenhearted,
And in Me is where you will find peace
of mind and rest for your weary soul.
Come ... for today I have determined unto you,
It is 'A Time for Love.'"

Set Apart

Prelude

How many of us disqualify ourselves when it comes to being used by God? How many of us do not believe that God has a purpose and a plan for our lives? We look at ourselves and because we cannot recognize the purpose of God, we do not see our value. We are all precious to God. We are all significant whether we believe it or not. It is a struggle sometimes to envision and say to ourselves, "I am a valuable and significant person." It may seem to some that this would be cocky or an arrogant assessment of self. However, you and I must see ourselves as God sees us. He desires to use every one of us if we are a willing vessel. Fears lead to apprehensions that prevent us from becoming truly what God has created us to be. Once in a while God will speak a few little words to you that are so powerful they stand you up on your feet and blow breath under your wings. Words just like these! I have an incredible expectation of God. I believe that He will do what He has spoken. You should too. I am grateful that He would consider me to do anything for Him on His behalf.

I the Lord your God created you,
To live an incredible life in me.
I set you apart from others,
I summoned you to search and find Me.

Believe Me when I declare a thing to you,
Trust in the words that I speak,
For every word is truth.
And never consider the words of another over Mine.

They do not know the thoughts I
hold in My mind for you.
They do not know the future I have prepared for you.
I am God and I alone am the One
who knows everything!
So believe in Me and believe in
the you I said you are.

You cannot look at your faults and walk with Me,
You will stumble.
You cannot look at your fears,
For you will certainly tremble.

But look at Me and what I have given you to succeed.
I have withheld from you nothing!
I have given you everything!
You are not without!

If you keep looking at yourself you will
never become what I expect.
And yes, I expect you to flourish.
Flourish into the fine masterpiece I see.
Let Me paint across the canvas of your life.

You are My signature piece, a prized possession!
So don't be afraid!
Trust and simply do what I say.
I set you apart ... Walk with Me.

Fingerprint

Prelude

I can see the hand of God throughout my life. As a child, I would lie on my bed in my room and ask God the question, "Where are You? I want to see You." I can see Him in my youth as a teen, visiting me in dreams, showing me things that I did not understand at the time. I understand now that they were set in the future. I see Him as a young adult giving me instruction in what to do and what not to do.

I was not always obedient, yet He continued calling my name and persuading me to come to Him. I can see Him in my adult life; He is a present help and a constant strength. He has helped, healed, delivered and prospered this child. He has been my supreme supporter. God has encouraged and advanced me to elevated heights and depths in Him. He has loved me like no other and has been here for me always. His peace and His comfort are beyond description. I do not know what I would do without Him. I see Him all over my life.

I recognize Your fingerprint throughout my days.
I can see Your indentations on my life,
And even now, I still see Your hand.
You have delivered me from my own wickedness.

You have displayed much mercy and grace.
Because of Your love for me,
You chose not to allow me to remain the same.
I see Your fingerprint.

How does one repay You?
For I cannot thank You enough,
For the correction, direction, and instruction.
There are not enough hallelujahs,
There are not enough amens,
For my salvation.
What can I word that would satisfy Your ear?
What do I have to give?
Yet, I see Your fingerprint.

For Your immeasurable love has overwhelmed me!
You are indescribably wonderful!
I am speechless in the arms of Your embrace!
And at Your whisper, I am made still.
Frightened sometimes in Your presence,
I am kissed with Your peace.
I see Your fingerprint.

For I am being romanced by the love of my life.
I said, "Yes to your dance."
So You continually teach me how to
step with You through life.
You teach me how to bow in humility.
You raise me up and elevate my thinking.
You move me according to Your melody.
Father, I see Your fingerprint.
I see Your fingerprint all over my life.

I am thankful!
I am grateful!
I acknowledge You!
I recognize You!
I bless You!
And I worship You!
I can identify Your hand upon my life!
I see Your fingerprint.

The Gift

Prelude

How many believe that when God birthed us into the earth, He did so with the intent of not only gifting our parents but gifting us as well. I do not know if we look at the extreme makeup of our being and appreciate the life God has given to us. We are all gifts! We really must enjoy the gift of life for which God has graced us. You are a gift of God. Take care of you, appreciate and love yourself. You are a beautiful present. Yes, you are! I did not ask you to consider what other people think. Think about what God thinks about you. He created you beautiful. Enjoy your life, take care of your gift and laugh at every opportunity you get. Life is too short, and the gift only remains for a small season.

You are a gift that God has given to you, yourself.
On the day that you were born,
God graced you with the "Gift of Life."
He breathed into your nostrils;
You became a living soul.

Your life is a gift.
Treasure it, love it, and celebrate it.
Let laughter be the instrument that centers it
And God be the One who brings balance to it.
Let your joy always be full.

For life is but a moment,
Like a vapor.
Like a whisper and it is gone.
Love hard.
Laugh hard, uncontrollably.
And live every day to the maximum.

God Knows

Prelude

God knows everything that we go through and all we endure. He knows us better than we know ourselves. He understands why we do what we do, when we cannot identify why we have done them. Have you ever asked yourself, "Why did I do that? Why did I say that? Why did I agree to that when I knew I didn't want to? Why did I sleep with that person? Why did I get divorced? Why did I get married? Why did I have children? Why did I not . . . ? Why do I love? Why can't I love? Why do I tell lies? Why do I stay on this job? Why, why, why?" Yes! Sure you have! We all have a "why" in our life. But God knows the why, and thank God He has and is the answer to the why. We need the help of God. Yes, we do!

God understands the reason why;
He understands the expressions in my life.
He is all that I have!
He doesn't judge me when I kneel before Him.
With my bruised heart in my hand,
He doesn't turn away from me.

He will have mercy on me.
He will help me.
He will correct me in my nakedness before Him.
He will take me by my hand and lift me to my feet.
He knows that I am in need of Him.
He knows that I cannot make it without Him.

I can trust Him with my mind,
I can trust Him with all my heart,
And I can trust Him with all the days of my life.
He knows me better than I know myself.
I am created by Him and exist because of Him.
I am because He is.

When I call on His name, He answers me.
I trust what He says.
He knows my every expression.
He is the One who understands.
He knows my reasons why,
And He helps me with my life.

Walking on Water

Prelude

I had a dream about my mother. She was lying limp in her bed. Her body began to slide like a mass of fluid. Before she hit the floor, I caught her. My sister called me and said I needed to come home because my mother was not being very responsive. When I arrived and looked at her, I understood the dream. She resembled what I had seen in the dream. Needless to say, we called 911. Immediately the ambulance responded, and she was taken into emergency at the hospital.

After a lengthy consultation with her personal physician regarding the procedures to save her life, she was subsequently taken into the Intensive Care Unit (ICU). He was not certain of the outcome and had given my sister and me the possibilities of what could potentially happen. Her physician explained that she may not make it, and we needed to prepare ourselves for the potential of that reality.

The presence of God is so awesome! He wrapped me all up in His peace. That is the only way I can explain what I was experiencing at the time. I literally felt as though I was walking above the ground and not on the ground at all. Every day I got up to go to the hospital, it felt like my feet were not touching the ground. I didn't know what was going to happen, but the peace of God engulfed me. The thing that amazes me the most is that it was not my decision to walk in this kind of peace, but it was God who elevated me to this place. I can't even tell you why He did it, He just did. He blessed me to trust Him! I physically felt Him hold me together.

My mom regained consciousness and God sustained her through her storm and blessed her to live. After several months of rehabilitation to regain muscle strength, she returned home with the assistance of my sisters, Bonnie, Erma, and Charle. She is currently eighty-six years old and still holding on to God's faithful hand. God is a wonderful and faithful God, and I am a very grateful child.

There is a place in God,
Where you can go,
A place where peace,
Really rules your soul.
You know God has it under control,
Though you cannot see,
What shall be.
Walking on water,
It's like walking on water,
Walking on water,
Your feet don't touch the ground.

I received a call,
That my mother was ill.
I spoke with the doctor;
He didn't know whether or not she would live.

I ran to my Father's house,
And I lay before Him,
He held me in His arms,
And said, "Child, just be still."
Walking on water,
It's like walking on water,
Walking on water,
My feet didn't touch the ground.

I went to the hospital.
There she lay,
Night after night and day after day.
I watched her blood pressure drop,
As well as her heart rate.
But inside I knew she wasn't
walking through the gate.
Walking on water,
It's like walking on water,
Walking on water,
My feet didn't touch the ground.

As time passed on,
Her strength grew.
I watched God do what only He could do.
He sustained her life,
And blessed her to live.
He heard the prayers that were sent.
Walking on water,
It's like walking on water,
Walking on water,
My feet didn't touch the ground.

Do This

Prelude

We all have things in our lives that we would like to not recall. For some, it is easier said than done. I remember when I was young and heard older people talk about how they regretted some of the things they had done in their life. Their right-now moment was hindered and anchored in past dissatisfaction. One foot was in the present, and one was shackled in the past. Their whole person was not carried forward into their right-now life. It seemed like they were caught between two periods of time, yesterday that did not exist anymore and the reality of today.

We cannot retrieve yesterday, and we cannot make up for time already spent, but we can learn from the good, the bad, the hurt, and the pain. Forgive yourself, forgive others and live in your now moment. If you can make something better, do it from where you are now, not where you were. You are no longer there!

How can you see what God has before you when your head is continually turned around in the past? The past is a time forgotten, a season that is done away with, accumulated moments that reflect a time that cannot be gathered together or recaptured again. It is time that is spent. Whether spent wisely or foolishly, it is gone. Stop regretting and reflecting upon your faults, what man is without them? Learn from them and move on.

Forgive yourself and forgive others and please, please stop second-guessing what you know God has called you to become. It is a devise of the enemy to have your mind so convoluted with past discrepancies that you cannot focus on the future God has prepared before you. When God forgave you, He forgave you! He does not remind you of who you were and what you did before Jesus Christ came and transformed your life. So release the past, turn your head forward, hear God, put one foot in front of the other, and press toward the mark. God has richly invested in you!

God for Sale

Prelude

There are men and women whom God has endowed with great wisdom and given revelation of who He is. God has entrusted them with what He has disclosed. They are gifted in the wisdom and revelation of God. They have endured suffering and hardship, and in the midst of their trial God has manifest Himself faithful on their behalf. It is the reward of a sacrificed life to God. It is the God experience. They have been privileged to witness God's power. God has proven Himself to be who He declared.

Some have placed a price tag on the revelation God has entrusted them with. God commissioned the believer to go out and tell the world about who He is. He did not say go out and charge the world for the information of God. The revelation of God may have cost you, but it is not to be charged to the people you give it to. Obey God and be blessed!

I gave you My gifts without repentance.
I will not recall them back to Me.
They were placed in you to shine in the world,
To be a light to men,
To give Me glory in the land.

But you sell them like a prostitute.
You charge when you should be
rendering them freely.
You too will have to stand before Me.
What will you say?
What will be your reason for selling
the King's treasures so cheaply?

I am not for sale!
Yet My words are being sold.
Is it not I who gave you the wisdom?
Is it not I who gave you the insight?
Is it not I who opened your mind to understand Me?

The people are in need of what you know,
But they cannot afford you.
I am not to be sold!
You are to freely tell of who I am,
Give the gift I have placed within you.

How will the poor learn of Me?
Are they not worthy of what you
have received from Me?
To the highest one who bids for you, you come.
You sell yourself, yet you are My treasure.
What answer are you prepared to give Me?

You will have to pay!
You will have to pay!

The Unknown Inheritance

Prelude

God presented this poetic writing in the form of a question. When I thought about God's perspective, I realized that it would be more than disappointing if I had written an inheritance to someone I love, and they never opened the letter to know what it read. It would grieve me to know that I had awarded them everything, but they remained in the same critical condition prior to the award of inheritance. Wealthy but living poor, free but living bound. I think I would be more than saddened. I would be truly devastated! Knowing that I had provided for every need within their life, yet they were ignorant to the ownership of their rightful possession.

How much do you think God loves us? He has made every way for us clear through His Son, Jesus Christ. He has given us a lavish inheritance. God's passion for us is incredible and awesome. He loves us so much. I ask these questions to both you and me: Do we really know what the heart of God is for us? Have we grasped an understanding of our Kingdom inheritance? Do we perceive what He has left in our possession? Who we are in Him; do we get it? We must know His Word and what He has said about Himself, as well as what He has said about you and me. We are to live above only, but how can we if we do not have the prescription, which is found in His Word?

If you wrote many letters,
And gave them to Me,
And I never opened them to see what they read,
How would that make you feel?
Would you be sad?
To know I would never know for Me
What you have said.

If you made Me promises,
That you did keep,
And I never heard you give your word to Me,
How would it make you feel?
Would you be sad?
To know I would never know for Me
Your words of promise you've kept.

If you gave Me the keys to life,
And unlocked all the doors,
And made every way clear for Me,
And the path was sure,
How would it make you feel?
Would you be sad?
To know you've conquered everything,
But your children are still oppressed.

On the pages of the "Book of Life,"
There are written letters for your life.
Therein lay your life's plan.
But how can you understand?

How can you ever become,
The reason for what I have done,
When you have not heard,
Because you have not read My Word!

It's All Just Temporary

Prelude

I believe there is a place in God through faith, relationship and the study of His Word that you realize this world is just temporary and you are eternal. It changes your perspective on life. As I consider how all these things shall pass, I pondered on the thought of my soul living forever. Forever does not have time attached, it is endless. We have a choice of where we shall spend eternity. I respect this magnificent reality and recognize this shall all pass away.

This is a temporary place,
With a temporary body,
In temporary time.

The kingdom of God is a permanent place,
With a permanent body,
In permanent time.

This present life is subject to limits of time.
Set in parameters.
This "time in space" will not last,
but the kingdom has no end!
It is eternal, forever existing.

I must be acutely aware of this truth.
It is not my truth, but rather the truth of God.
For that which I see shall not be as I have known it,
And that which I do not see, shall be beyond
that which I can dream, forever established!

I am in this place with my physical body,
Yet, I am in the kingdom with my spirit.
I am in this world, but not of this world.
And I must align myself with that reality.

I must live my life in agreement with the expectation,
That has been established for me by God.
For truly the kingdom is eternal,
And this is all just temporary.

Journey

Prelude

You never know what shall happen within your day. Something can take place that you never saw coming and catch you off guard. Because you are not anticipating what occurs it has the ability to cause a temporary sting of confusion. You do not have an immediate answer to the question, "Why?" I found myself in such a situation when removed unexpectedly from a position for no apparent reason. The explanation or reason that was given to me was that I was excellent in my job performance, and I was a testimony unto myself.

I thought, *Wow! What a smoke screen.* Although, I personally did not appreciate being removed; in reality, it was God's timing for me to leave. I needed to trust God for the change and trust where He was about to take me. God was using that individual to cause me to move forward. God really does work everything out for the good of those who love Him and are called according to His purpose. You have to trust Him for your journey even if you don't understand what He is doing. Trust God because He sees and He knows what He has in store for your future.

I'm not gon'na let you take my smile from me.
I'm not going to let you take my joy.
I'm not gon'na be sorry, no not today.
Cause God has something more for me.
I must leave now to go and see.
And I cannot be afraid.

Every step I take is ordered of the Lord.
Every move I make is Him.
In Him I live, I breathe, and I am because He is.
I must go where I've never gone.
Do the things I've never done.
I will have to trust Him through it all.

So I ain't gon'na let nobody take my smile from me.
I'm not going to let anyone take my joy.
I will not let someone break God's Spirit in me.
For this is what the Lord has given.
To Him, I owe all the praise.
And I want Him to be satisfied.

I ain't gon'na let nobody take what God's given me.
Can't surrender anything, anyway.
He's invested too much, poured too much in me.
So I am on a journey now.
Don't even want to figure how.
All I want to do is just obey!

In One Moment

Prelude

We do silly things without thinking about the consequences, and when we disobey God, we pay the price for our disobedience. God is faithful to forgive us when we ask, but we must still suffer the results of the act. This hymn was written to remind me of the consequences of those choices paid over a lifetime for a decision that could be made in a single moment. When I look through my past, I realize that I have made enough of them, and some I will hate forever because they did not contribute anything to my life. Thank God Almighty for His Word that taught me to forget those things that were behind me and press toward the mark of the higher calling in Christ Jesus.

The decisions you make in a moment's time can cause your feet to carry your whole body to a place God never intended. At the end of that road, you consider the trial you inflicted upon yourself and pose this question, "How in the hell did I get here?"

Making the right choices at a moment's notice is crucial; it will determine the degree of contentment you will have in rest of your life.

In one moment,
Your life can change,
By one decision that you make,
And all you've done is now in vain,
In just one moment.
In just one moment!

In one moment,
One thing you do,
Can change the course God has for you,
And the troubles you shouldn't have to go through,
In just one moment,
In just one moment!

That is why God said,
"Get your mind renewed.
Walk in the Spirit so the flesh can be subdued.
And all I have invested in you,
It won't be lost!
It won't cost you in one moment."

In one moment,
The price you to pay,
Can be charged to the rest of your days.
With regret, you say,
"If I'd only done it God's way."
In just that one moment.

Distractions

Prelude

Have you ever sat back and observed favoritism in the workplace? It can be rather disturbing, especially when it is so crisp, clear, and blatant. Sometimes you see things that are not right, but unfortunately there isn't anything you can do based on how the favoritism is manipulated. You know it, and it is evident, but you cannot prove it. Everyone involved is within an inner circle and cover one another. If you are not someone who participates in the internal networking of the powers to be, you are an excluded person.

You have to submit these questions to yourself: Are you willing to pay the asking price to be included? What must you surrender? What do you have to give, now or later? You are going to sacrifice something, and this kind of sacrifice is not for the glory of God. This sacrifice may be your integrity, your dignity, your self-respect, your self-worth, your moral values, your husband, your wife, or your children. I have watched people surrender themselves to be a part of someone's click and lost more than what they thought they were going to gain!

As I noticed the blatant favoritism, as well as promises given that were fulfilled, God brought to my attention that I was giving all of this too much consideration. It was definitely disturbing to watch. I must say that I was rather astonished at how transparent things were done, many times over.

I was distracted by the behaviors of men and thank God that He brought this to my attention. God reminded me that it is He who causes men to rise and it is He who causes men to fall, and every one of them has their place for only a limited season.

I have caused you to reign above your circumstances,
To observe your conditions from above;
But if you are not careful to abide in your place,
You will be dragged into the midst of issues.
How can you see clearly in the midst?

When you are eye to eye with the circumstances,
They are all you notice,
All that you are capable of seeing.
You are consumed by them,
And they have become greater than you.

Now you find yourself beneath them.
They have stepped on your neck,
Instead of you stepping on the neck of the issue.
You have been given power and authority.
You are seated in high places with all spiritual gifts.

Stay with Me!
You will find that My Word will
pull you up, out and over,
And sustain you to remain in your proper place.
But you must agree with Me,
You are above only.

For I have caused you to reign
above your circumstances,
To observe conditions from above
only and not beneath.

I Don't Know Why

Prelude

When I meditate on the Lord and think about how good He is, I cannot come up with any reason for Him to cover me or consider me as He does. Truly, it is nothing that I have done. It moves me to bless Him, to love Him and to worship. His love is true, pure and absolutely unexplainable. I still don't know why He loves me so much. This is the love of my Father.

Lord, I glorify Your name.
No one is the same,
I glorify Your name.
There is no one else like You.
Who does the things You do, for me.
You would not let me stay the same,
You called me by my name,
And showed me Your way.

Lord, I glorify Your name.
No one is the same
I glorify Your name.
Oh! How! You were the sacrifice,
You suffered your life.
I can't repay!
You saved me from the grave.
Beyond the dust I live,
Because of what you did.

Lord, I glorify Your name.
No one is the same;
I glorify Your name.
As I look back over my years,
You've always held me near.
You kept me for Yourself,
To fall in love with no one else.
I don't know why?
You've covered my life ...

Thank You

Prelude

When you have been a consistent giver and become exhausted in your labor of love, you appreciate when your husband, wife, children, boss, or whoever you think is significant in your life, gives you a simple thank you. You value those two little words so much. So how much more does God welcome and appreciate our words when we simply acknowledge Him with a thank you? We know that God does not tire, for He is not flesh but spirit. Yet God does everything for us. I humbly choose to acknowledge Him and to let Him know that I am grateful. The poem expresses missed moments of opportunity. It is never too late to give Him thanks, especially when you are still above the ground.

If I haven't talked to You lately,
If I haven't recognized,
If I haven't even noticed,
My eyes have been blind.
I want to take this opportunity,
To say with all my heart,
With all my soul,
And with my entire mind,
Lord, I thank You!

If I haven't shown my affection,
If I haven't praised Your name,
If our intimacy is suffering,
And I am to blame,
I want to take this opportunity,
To say with all my heart,
With all my soul,
And with my entire mind,
Lord, I thank You!

Lord, I am grateful
For Your shadow that covers me.
I am grateful for Your Word that instructs me.
I am grateful for Your Spirit that leads me.
I am thankful for the fellowship.
You've been so good to me.
I'm grateful, Lord, for all You have done,
And all that You continue to do for me.

Go On

Prelude

Remember this when you are going through a difficult time in your life: it is just that, a difficult time you are *going through.* Trials come to make you strong and reveal you to yourself. You do not know what your true character or strength is until you have gone through hardship. You will understand the truth of who you are and what you are made of. Just remember this: God has equipped you with everything you need to be victorious.

There was a situation in my life regarding my finances. It was a difficult time and I couldn't see the light of day, dim or bright. I relied on God's Word and did not cease to fervently pray and faithfully return my tithe. My situation was not transformed immediately.

It took some time, I must admit, for things to turn around. Little by little, God assisted me. During this process I learned the importance of being a good steward over my finances. A meaningful lesson I learned that would last longer than the duration of my adversity. My attitude about my situation was drastically changed, and God blessed me through it! God gave me the wisdom I needed. So you see, there is a light at the end of the tunnel. You may not be able to see it immediately; however, it is there to guide you through the dark moments. God will give you what you need to get through. Stay with Him and trust Him, and where there are uncertainties in your life, you will see God place your feet on solid ground!

No matter what it looks like,
I've got to go on,
No matter what I feel,
I've got to be strong.
Everything I want,
It doesn't always come my way.
And the cares of this world,
Are sometimes very weighty.

No matter how my heart hurts,
And cuts so deeply,
No matter how my mind seems,
Seems to trouble me.
I thank the Lord above,
For giving me an escape.
If it wasn't for the Lord,
There isn't much that I could take.

I have a Savior that cares about me.
The lover of my soul cares about my needs.
He holds me close,
He is comforting.
When I ask of Him,
He answers me.
He knows me by name,
And in Him I am not ashamed.

It isn't always easy to walk with the Lord.
It isn't always easy to be in one accord.
The enemy is lurking to deceive me,
With false gratifications to attempt to please,
And challenge my mind to doubt the love of God,
Especially when times are hard,
I must hold fast to His unchanging hand,
And wait on Him to give me strength to stand.

For Myself

Prelude

I have watched men and women who are the "children of the living God." They are peculiar, different. There is something extraordinary that exists between them and the One who created them. There is a union between them and God. Not only do you notice it displayed in their lives, but you can hear it in the sound of their voices when they speak. From my close observation of their lives, I wanted to know God for myself. I wanted my own exclusive relationship with Him. I began to search for Him, and 'til this day I remain in constant pursuit of Him. God is beyond my human capacity to articulate. The more I seek Him, the more I find Him. But I cannot sum Him with any combination of words. He is more than I can express, and I am drawn to know Him so much more.

I do not want to know You through someone else.
I desire to know You for myself.
I've heard the preacher preach of You.
I heard my mother testify since my childhood too.
But now that I have grown,
I don't want to journey alone.

Who are You?
Why have You loved me so much?
I can feel Your passion for me.
I can feel the gravity of Your affection draw me.
Yet, Your presence frightens me;
Yes, I know I must come.

I must hear You speak.
I must know the sound of Your voice.
I must know what You Word.
I must recognize You,
And acknowledge You instantly,
That I am led by Your Spirit.

I must know You for myself,
Not through someone else.
I've heard the preacher preach of You,
I've heard the teacher teach too,
I've heard the prophet prophesy.
But there is something stirring deep
down within me inside.

So day after day I do run,
To knock upon Your door.
Into the chamber of Your heart, you let me in,
To discover You more than the day before.
I cannot grasp it all.
So to You, I run again and again and again.

To know You for myself.

You Can See Jesus

Prelude

The Bible teaches us that God is evidenced by the things that are clearly seen. In other words, His invisible attributes are clearly seen in the things that He has made. God spoke it and the Word performed what God said. We can see God in everything—if we pay attention. His creations are wondrous! Do you ever take the time to just look at anything He has created and how fascinating it is? I do all the time, I can't help it. God leaves us without an excuse of His true existence. When I look around, I can see God everywhere.

Any day you can see Jesus,
In all the things that He has made.
There is nothing made that He did not create.
And all that is testifies of Him.
Open your eyes and you can see Him too.

The sun that lights up the morning sky,
The midnight moon that gleams
throughout the night.
You can see him in a baby's eyes,
In the tears that form when a child cries.
I can see Him in you.

He leaves us without excuse.
For by that which is seen,
He manifests His invisible attributes,
His eternal power and divine nature,
He testifies of Himself by the things He has created.

The birds that fly by,
The clouds that drop rain from up high,
A cow that says, "Moo,"
The wonderful fragrance in a flower bloom,
The breath of God in you.

Any day, you can see Jesus,
If you would open your eyes.

Chosen

Preface

At times, there are words that stir like the wind in your spirit. From out of nowhere and from no particular place, God chooses to talk to you just because there is something He desires to share with you. It isn't because of anything you have done or not done. It's one of those "just because" moments with God. It is just because of His love that He desires to communicate His heart to you. Just because …

I have called you out for this time and this season,
To represent Me and My kingdom.
I have called you to places you have never been,
To see things you have never seen,
And to reveal them to the people whom I love.

Have faith and fret not!
Know that I am here with you always.
Let your confidence be sound in Me,
Knowing that I, the Lord, have called you,
To many splendid and wondrous things.

Be not afraid;
The adversary will fight against you.
Darkness does not delight in the light.
But I have overcome all dark things!
And you are hid in Me.
Do My will!

I Miss You

Preface

I don't think we believe God to be one who misses our presence. If God made us in His image, and He did. Why would He not miss the presence of His loved ones? We miss the company of the people we love, don't we?! God desires our presence because He genuinely loves us? Do you spend time with God? I am sure He desires to spend time with you. Maybe the affairs in your life diminished the reality of your need for relationship with Him. Do you spend less time with Him compared to how you once did, if you did? I know interactions can rob you of your time with God. Your time with Him must be deliberate and intentional. I can surely say, "I know I am not the only one He misses!"

I miss you coming to My throne today.
I miss you entering into My
presence with your praise.
I miss you singing to Me a sweet melody.
I miss your voice.

There was so much I wanted to say;
There were some new things I needed
to give you, for this day.

But you didn't stop by, you didn't drop
by, there was no time for Me.
I miss your voice.

I desire to spend the time,
That we shared together,
In one moment in one mind.
I desire your presence before My throne.
Why have you left Me and gone?

You don't have time for Me anymore.
You are so caught up in the world's daily chores.
Why must I wait, anticipate?
I miss your voice!

I have always been right here for you,
To see you through all life's issues.
Come to Me, I hold the answers that you need.
I miss your voice!

I miss your voice!
I miss your voice!
I miss your voice!

Come to Him

Prelude

I remember being in a relationship with someone that I just flat-out adored. He was handsome, funny and fun to be around. There was only one problem: he didn't think the same of me. I was not the girl of his dreams! Our last telephone conversation was devastating! It usually is when you are the lover but not the loved, and the loved says, "I don't want to see you anymore."

I picked my heart up off the ground and carried it in my hands and laid it before God. It's funny because it isn't like the pain just went away. I was still hurt and embarrassed. I even felt ashamed. But the more I returned to God and declared my need for Him and the more I petitioned Him to help me, He did! As time progressed, the sting in my heart faded. God healed my heart and restored my peace. I have learned through experience that God will heal and replenish your spirit if you will simply ask. He has proven His faithfulness over and over again. Ask Him for whatever you need. He is faithful to deliver.

When your heart has been broken into pieces,
And the pieces are trampled on the ground,
And in the cloak of darkness, the
tears pour like a heavy rain,
And you cannot see life through the severity of pain,

God is here for you;
He's watching what you are going through.
His compassion delights in helping you,
And His love longs to undergird you.

He desires that you would come to Him,
For He knows this is not your end.
Although you feel that it is.
He has something more to give.

There isn't anything that He cannot do for you.
His compassion and love will strengthen you.
He will cause you to overcome,
And make you to rise like the morning sun.

God will wipe the tears from your eyes,
Interrupt your troubled thoughts,
and put peace in your mind.
And that broken heart that you
thought would never heal,
God will wrap you in His arms
and heal what you feel.

He knows what you go through.
He traveled this road long before you.
He is acquainted with hurt and with pain;
He has suffered humiliation and shame.

So lay all your cares at His feet,
And declare to Him what you need.
He is willing and more than able
to dry your weeping eyes,
And repair the damaged pieces inside.

Come to Him!

My Word

Prelude

Some years ago, I heard this hymn in my spirit. When I heard it, I was shaken by it because I know anything you receive from God is something he actually gives to *you.* It is initially intended for the recipient! You must process it thoroughly before you even consider trying to share it with someone else. So I had to address myself and ask myself the question, "Do I believe God's Word? Not only do I believe His Word, but do I believe what He has said about me in His Word?" I have to admit, no, I did not! I say this because after considering and contemplating my trust in God, I had to ask myself, "Do I trust Him or am I just saying I trust Him." I mean, trust Him with my life, my whole life, my dreams, my aspirations, my future. Do I trust Him with the sum of all that I am?

I realized there were some things I did not trust Him with. There were matters I was afraid to trust Him with and trust Him for. What I discovered to be most interesting was once again. God brought it to my attention. God is consistent in making you aware of your shortcomings. He lovingly does so to ensure you do not overlook His wonderful blessings. Imagine that! I thank God for His grace! In my journey, He has and is still teaching me how to trust Him at His Word and come into agreement with what He has spoken about me, as well as Himself. I have not attained the depth in God I so desire, but I have measured growth from where I have come. I know and am confident that He who began a good work in me will see it to the finish. That is His promise!

You don't believe My Word.
Even though you've heard it, you don't believe it.
You don't believe what I've said about Me,
And you don't believe what I've said about you.
No, you don't believe it!
You can't receive it!
My Word.

Who do you think I am?
Do you think I cannot perform what I said I can?
Where is your faith and trust in Me?
To believe the Words I've spoken,
That set you free?
But you don't believe!
You can't receive!
My Word.

I've made provisions in what I have given,
So you can walk in the power of Me.
All that I am, I've placed in your hands.
You have everything in you that you will ever need.
I have held nothing back.
You are perfect in Me.
But you must believe it!
You must receive it!
My Word.

I endured the humiliation;
I endured the pain.
They stretched Me out naked,
And I endured the shame.
Do you think it was all nothing?
I paid a price to set you free,
That in Me, by Me, and through Me,
You have the victory.
But you must believe it!
You must receive it!
My Word.

Keep Me

Preface

God is so awesome; He will never leave you where you began. The more time I spend with God, the more of Him He reveals. The more time I spend with Him, the more He exposes the truth about me. The more I seek Him, the more He draws me to find Him. God will never allow you to remain stagnant. He is constantly teaching you and me in order to develop us into true sons and build us in every aspect of our lives.

He is perpetual in His call to draw you deeper into His presence to reveal truths and hide you in Himself. God's love is relentless. You are His work in progress. You are the workmanship of His hands, and it is His intention to keep you for Himself.

You drew me near to You,
To hear the truth,
And teach me how to live,
Right here with You.
I didn't understand Your stretched-out, caring hand,
The love You poured on me,
Was more than I had believed.
I pray to stay with You;
Yes, I pray to stay with You, my Lord.

You've brought me closer now,
To know Your ways,
And though I was afraid of You,
I came anyway.
Your presence frightened me.
I fell down on my knees.
You touched me with Your peace,
And stood me to my feet.
I pray to stay with You!
Yes, I pray to stay with You, my Lord.

You've shown mysteries I had never known,
The deep hidden things,
That only You can show.
You instructed me,
In truth I did not see.
You constantly lead me,
And teach me how to walk eternally.

So, I pray to stay with You, my Lord.
Yes, I pray to stay with You, my Lord.
I pray to stay with You!
I pray to stay with You!

Into Your Arms

Prelude

As I think about the presence of God and reflect on how comforting it is, there isn't anything I cannot carry to Him and lay at His feet. He is so compassionate and willing to hear about my every need.

When you enter into His presence, He will lift you from His feet and hold you in His arms. What He tells you while He is holding you will be words that will sustain and strengthen you. There is power in His Word, and in His Word is life. His comforting love makes me want to run to Him. It makes me want to run!

I want to run to You.
Fall into Your arms,
Is what I long to do.
Feel the power of Your sweet embrace,
As you hold me in Your arms,
Cheek to cheek,
And face-to-face,
I want to run.

To be with You,
Is what my heart anticipates looking forward to,
To touch You once again,

As You draw me near,
To speak life into my ear,
Cheek to cheek,
And face-to-face,
I want to run.

There is no place else that I would rather be.
Lying on Your breast,
Listening to Your heart beating,
Telling me things I've never heard,
Listening intently to Your every Word.
Cheek to cheek,
And face-to-face,
I love to run.

Love Affair

Preface

Consider your life! Stop for a moment and turn around to examine the miles of road you have covered. Contemplate all that has been good, bad and indifferent in your life; you can see God. The reality of God's involvement is undeniable. You recognize that it has been God who has kept you, covered you and sweetly loved you all the days of your life. My heart questions—Why? "Why have you been so good to me God? Why are you so wonderful to me?" The love of God is too much to be measured and too deep to be understood.

Father, You are such an awesome and mighty God.
You continually take care of me.
All of my problems and issues, You oversee them.
You watch me!
I know that You watch over me.

I can sense Your presence,
And I can feel Your touch.
I often wonder why,
Why do You treat me as though
I am someone special?
I know that I am loved and You
are no respecter of persons.

You have held me in Your arms,
Kissed me on my cheek,
Whispered in my ear,
Awakened me,
You have awakened me.

You share pieces of Your heart.
Parts of Your mind,
And I am mesmerized,
At the revelation of what You express.
You are astonishing.

You have brought me into such an
intimate relationship with You.
It is incomparable, unimaginable, and so unnatural.
You have captivated my heart,
And become a wonder to my soul.
And I am in awe.

The Mark of the Beast

Preface

There have been moments when I have heard songs or poetic writings at the most awkward times. I would grab a pen and find a piece of paper to write down what I was hearing. I remember crossing an intersection on my way home from work and scrambling to find paper and pen, which I did. So, I drove with a piece of paper in one hand while on the steering column and wrote with the other. It was the second time this had occurred. I know that it sounds dangerous, but traffic was slow, and I was traveling on a country road. I had to capture the moment; if not, I would have lost the original thought. So here we are.

The mark of the beast is drawing nigh.
What will you do?
Will you choose death or life?
I hear the footsteps of the Lord draw near,
Making His last appeal,
To all of them who will give an ear.

I hear the Word say,
"When men cry peace,
There shall come sudden destruction."
I hear the Word say,

"When you see these things,
Know that I am at your door,
I will take no more."

The red heifers are being prepared,
Abomination …
To be sacrificed in the temple over there.
A man who comes in his own name.
Who will embrace him?
And have their soul utterly destroyed and shamed?

I hear the Word say,
"When men cry peace,
There shall come sudden destruction."
I hear the Word say,
"When you see these things,
Know that I am at your door,
I will take no more."

You cannot serve two masters.
You will love the one,
Or you will hate the other.
Your soul can still be saved.
Repent and turn away,
Turn from your wicked, wicked ways.

I hear the Word say,
"When men cry peace,
There shall come sudden destruction."
I hear the Word say,
"When you see these things,
Know that I am at your door,
I will take no more."

Be a Doer

Prelude

I have no desire to take a book, song or poem to the grave! Everything that God has gifted me to do, I want it completed. Every dream, aspiration and every vision that God has given me, I want them to remain in the earth. I do not want anything in the grave that does not belong there. Everything that is useful to men and gives God glory; I pray to accomplish. In order to achieve my purpose, I cannot waste my time or spend time with people who do not value my time or theirs. Your time equals your life. Once your time is up, guess what? So is your life!

You must take advantage of every moment in every day and make it count for whatever dream or aspiration God has set in your spirit. Do not think that you are too young or too old. If God put it in you, He put it in you to give Him glory, to be blessed and be a blessing to humanity. Do not procrastinate; that is time wasted you could have purposely invested into your future. *Do the do!* It's up to you to be all God created you to be! Stop talking! Put your words into action and walk into the destiny God has ordained. Be a doer!

Speak no more, be silent.
Perform that which you have declared you can do.
Stop procrastinating and wasting God's time.
Let your words be moved into action.

Secure your opportune moment.
For tomorrow is not promised.
Today belongs to you.
Take advantage of every opportunity.

You have talked long enough.
The works of your hands show no proof.
Now do what you said you can.
It is still day.

For no man can work from the grave.
He is done.
The memory dwindles after.
The mind cannot capture what
he has not left behind.

Spend life wisely.
Your allotted time is all you have.
Do what you say.
Make your words and actions agree.

Press Your Way

Prelude

Do you ever contemplate how much others endure? Or how much you have endured in your own life? I was considering the lives of people. Everyone has some sort of heartache in life—if you have not, keep living. There is a trial on the horizon waiting for you; it is a part of life! The Word of God teaches that trials come to make you strong. How will we ever identify what we are made of, capable of, or what kinds of strengths or weakness we have if we are never tested for anything? If you are suffering through a trial, know that God is with you and will give you the ability to press all the way to the other side of victory. Your testimony of the greatness of God awaits you. Hold on to God! He will see you through.

There are times when life gets so hard,
Down here on this earth we are walking on.
Sometimes you want to give up,
Finding it difficult to press your way.
Strife, tribulation, spiritual warfare,
Your faith is tried every day.

The only thing that keeps me going on,
Are the promises Christ has made to me.

The security of His promises keeps me strong,
Knowing He has gone to prepare a place for me,
A place where I shall spend eternity,
As I anticipate His return for me.

But Satan tries to give you things,
Wicked, deceitful, sly things,
To carry your soul straight to hell with him,
And vigorously try to overthrow
God's intent for you to live.
He knows what his end shall be,
And he knows heaven is your destiny.

He doesn't want you to go,
To a place he can never return.
There is another place prepared for him to burn.
He'll make your life hard.
You can never let down your guard.
God has placed everything in you
to press your way through.

Remember, the race is not given to the swift,
Nor the battle to the strong,
But to him that endures all things till the end.
Be of good courage,
Let your faith not waiver,
And know that God is fulfilling all of His promises.

Return

Prelude

It is a fantastic reality when you are in an intimate relationship with God. Sensing His presence is easy. It is not hard, difficult, or a strain to access Him. He is here! When you open your mouth to worship, He is here. You think about God and tears swell in your eyes and roll down your cheeks because at the thought of Him, just at the thought, you are provoked to touch Him with your worship.

I found myself asking God one day, "How did I lose my intimacy with You? How did I find myself in this place? How did I become contrary? I am a worshiper!" I realized that I had begun praying without touching God, and my prayer life had become routine. I had lost my passion. My enthusiasm and expectancy had gradually slipped away. This was something else God brought to my attention. The truth is; God makes us aware of all things. It was God who opened my mind to reflect upon me. I am telling you, God will not allow you to remain the same.

During this season in my life, I thought I was fine. I was not conscious of how far I had drifted from the lover of my soul. That is frightening! God said, "You need to return to Me." I am so grateful to know God will never leave me nor forsake me. He will not permit my heart to be misplaced outside of His. If I have lost my aim, and I am moving backward instead of forward; His love will draw me into His arms again. If it was not for His love, mercy and grace, where would I be? Lord, "Where would I be?"

I want to return to You,
My heart, my soul, my mind.
Through the storm and the rain,
Through the clouds and the pain,
I lost my way and could not see,
That You were standing right here with me.

I want to return to You,
My heart, my soul, my mind,
it all belongs to You.
The battle has been tough,
At times, I have missed You, God,
Your voice that was so clear,
I heard whispering in my ear.

I want to return to You,
My heart, my soul,
My life I submit to You.
I miss the warmth of Your embrace,
The getaway to our secret place,
You waking me in the middle of night,
Just to say, "You want some time."

I return myself to You;
I give myself back to You.
My heart, my soul, my mind,
I give it all back.

My heart, my soul, my mind,
I return to You.
I give me, all back to You, O God!

Romance

Preface

I was reclining at my kitchen table early one morning as I was sipping a cup of herbal tea. As I sat looking out of my glass door, I heard the birds begin their melody. (I love listening to the birds sing.) It triggered my thoughts about the magnificent beauty of God. As I considered His majesty, this little song came to mind. God is a God of romance. He will serenade you with His presence and awesome love. Let Him.

Ain't nothing like the early morning,
Sitting with God.
There is nothing like the early morning,
Waking to His love.

Ain't nothing like feeling,
The power of His touch,
Sipping on a cup of tea,
In the presence of the Majesty,
Singing Him a melody.

There is nothing like it,
There's nothing like it,
Ain't nothing like,
Just sitting with God.

Hold On

Prelude

When I first met my husband, he was dashing, handsome, and lovely; he still is. During the course of our dating relationship, I set him on a pedestal. As time passed, he picked me up, turned me upside down, and dropped me on top of my head. He was lovely, but he was not perfect. He had his own set of challenges in his life. His greatest challenge was his fear of falling in love with me, which is funny because he already was but too afraid to submit to the power of love.

Twenty-five years later, we laugh about our trial-and-error beginnings. But by no stretch of the imagination was it funny at the time. The first few years of our marriage was likened to a roller coaster ride. I wanted to get off! Stop the car! I want to get out! He and I decided in order for our marriage to work, we were going to have to serve and trust God. We both desired the will of God in our lives and hoped in Him to mature us in our marriage. God really did work it out and continues to work in our Holy matrimony. Today my husband is still as dashing, handsome and lovely as ever. He is the most beautiful person I know. He really is beautiful! He still isn't perfect, but I appreciate what God has done and is still doing in his life as well as mine. We did not come thus far without some hurdles and obstacles, but I am grateful that we decided to trust God for the end results. We do have a sweet and passionate relationship, but that is because of the God we serve. To Him I owe all the glory!

Sometimes you bear things,
You really don't want.
They break your heart,
And tear your mind all apart.
It turns your life upside down,
And takes your feet right up off the ground.

But if you just hold out,
To just see what the end is going to be,
God will strengthen you, deliver you,
and refresh you, you'll see.

It can get to the point,
Where it looks so bad.
And you think to yourself,
There is no hope where I am.
Your vision for your life has shattered like glass.
You have forgotten who lifts your head.

But if you just hold out,
To just see what the end is going to be,
God will strengthen you, deliver you,
and refresh you, you'll see.

You know that every time you are going through,
God stands on the other side calling for you.
Christ is interceding on your behalf.
The Holy Spirit is leading you, like a guiding hand.

In your most difficult times, He will
undergird you to say, "Yes I can."

So just hold on,
See what the end is going to be.
God will strengthen you, deliver you,
and refresh you, you'll see.

He did it for me!

Expectations

Prelude

When Christ died, He left us an inheritance. This afforded each of us with unlimited opportunities to establish an individual intimate relationship with God through Christ Jesus. Christ not only made a way for us to personally walk with God but became the way in which we are to walk with Him. He gave us power, authority and all spiritual gifts that enable us to express what is expected of us. We are a magnificent people, and our inheritance gives us the right to satisfy the heart of God by living in the expectation of what He delights in.

There is an expectation I have of you.
It is not a single thing but many.
I expect you to give Me what I want.
For I have created you in My image.
You are a reflection of who I am.

I expect you to do good for evil.
I expect you to love your enemies.
I expect you to pray for those
who despitefully use you.
I expect you to forgive your brother over and over.
I expect you to tell people of who I AM.

I expect you to walk with Me,
So close that you can hear Me whisper,
And recognize My voice in a room filled with people,
Perk your ear and acknowledge that it is I,
And listen to what I command.

I expect you to commune with Me.
I expect the fellowship.
I expect you to come to Me with all your concerns,
And problems in life,
That I may help you sort through them.

I expect you to seek Me out!
I expect you to seek My counsel.
I expect you to ask questions.
I expect you to expect an answer.
And I expect you to pray for others, as yourself.

I have many expectations of you,
For you are a child of the King.
And I expect you to live a life that glorifies Me!
That in all your days you may live
an abundant and good life.
I have equipped you with everything
you need to satisfy Me.
There is an expectation I desire to see.

Seek Him Early

Prelude

You must find your perfect time with the Lord. A time when your mind is clear and not distracted with all the events that have occurred within your day. A time established for you and God alone. A time to hear and be heard.

I love the early morning, before the sun peaks over the horizon, before anyone has risen. I love it when my house is still and the business of the day has not yet begun. My mind is clear to hear and receive from the Lord without disturbance or interruptions. I enjoy the early morning with God.

Inquire of the Lord in all you do.
Seek Him early in the morning,
When it's just the two of you.
While the day is yet still,
Hear Him speak His will;
Catch the sound of His voice,
As He speaks into your ear.

Rise early in the morning,
Before your day becomes full.
Let Him be the first One that you kiss,
The first One you run to.

He delights in telling secrets,
With those who spend their time,
Revealing truths to empower your heart and mind.

Inquire of the Lord in all you do.
Seek Him early;
He is anticipating you.
Rise early in the morning,
Before the day breaks,
When silence is still lingering,
And you can hear what He has to say.

Seek Him early.

Judgment Day

Prelude

This poem kept echoing through my mind late one night while I was very tired and trying to retire for the evening. Since I couldn't sleep, I decided I better get up and write it down. I did not have a vision; I was trying to sleep, but based on the words I heard, I could imagine the event taking place.

What a horrible situation to find yourself in, thinking you have done what you believed was right, but you lacked what you needed to gain entrance into the kingdom of God. Here you stand before God after it is all said and done. He says, "You cannot go!" You have no recourse. What we do for Christ, according to the Word and the will of God, is what will speak on our behalf. We must be careful to obey God according to His pleasure, according to His will, and according to His purpose.

I had a vision one day,
Jesus came to take us away.
As He gathered us in,
One came running, saying, "Jesus, I'm coming."
He stood there naked and bare.
The Lord looked at him, and this is what He said:
He said, "You cannot go.

You had your chance; you did not follow,
You kept saying, 'Lord I'll come tomorrow.'"

Many were gathered around,
Saying, "Lord, Please look down.
Here I am; I'm the one who was the good person.
I gave money to the poor.
I gave to charities and did so much more."
He looked at them and said, "You cannot go!
You had your chance; you did not follow.
You kept saying, 'Lord, I'll come tomorrow.'"

Others were praying, others were saying,
"Lord, I accepted You,
As my Lord and my Savior too.
I did many things in your name.
You even forgave me for all of my shame."
He said, "You most of all, you,
You most of all cannot go.
You got saved and then you went astray,
And you never came back to me, no not one day."

Standing before Him

Prelude

Somehow we have come to believe that some sins are smaller than others or less noticeable. We have accepted the little white lie as being okay! It didn't really offend anyone. If we do not stop lying to ourselves and stop functioning in self-induced deceit, we are going to be some self-destructive, hell-bound people with no one to blame except ourselves. God has given us written instructions. It is our choice to follow the guidelines or not.

The last time I checked, a lie is still a lie and the truth is still the truth. There is no way around this reality. If you attempt to circumvent the truth, you lie to yourself. How we live in the earth will justify us or condemn us when we stand before God. He will judge all of us. No one is exempt! He does not need to speak a single word. His Word has already spoken on His behalf, and He will measure all of us according to it.

Sin is sin.
There is no such thing as a little sin or big sin.
There is no such thing as a little white lie.
A lie is a lie, for there is no truth inside of it.
It does not matter,
Whether it be the sin of adultery,

The sin of perversion,
The sin of promiscuity,
The sin of murder,
The sin of hate,
Or the sin of prejudice,
Or any sin that God has deemed as sin.
Our lives will unveil a testimony,
That will condemn us or justify us.

We will testify for or against our own life.
God need not speak a single word.
His Word has already spoken on His
behalf from the beginning.
All He needs to do is roll the tape of our lives.
And when we see ourselves on the screen of life,
We cannot point and falsely accuse God.
For our testimony will justify His
judgment against us,
Or deliver us from the wrath of
disobedience that waits.

For all sin is disobedience,
And all disobedience is missing the mark,
Not making the grade,
The inability to graduate from this temporary life,
To the eternal one which exists only in His kingdom.
For hell does not consist of life,
But the absence of love and everything living.
It is where dead things thrive,
And wickedness never ends.
Where there is no light, never
any light, just blackness.

We are not judged for sin we know not as sin.

Therefore, unknowingly we disobey
God out of our ignorance.
But the mercies of God will shine
light into our ignorance,
To expose us to ourselves,
That we might discontinue our sin against Him,
That brings judgment against us.
We must all stand before God and give an account,
From the time He blew breath into our nostrils,
Until the day we stand before Him.
We are all unmistakably accountable.

The Voice

Prelude

Never let the voice of another speak louder to you than the Word of God. Remember every word or thought that exalts itself above the Word of God; you cast it down. Cast it from your ears as well as your mind. Cast it from your life! Do not allow it room to breathe and smother the information God has given you regarding Him and you. You will always have people who desire to discredit the Word of God and will say, "You are crazy for believing in that book." It is not just believing in that book but rather believing in what is contained on the pages of the book. This book, the Bible, is the one and only that offers you something that no other book is able to propose; a better and more abundant life now and an eternal life later; made with a promise in blood. Do not give room for any devil, demon, or human being to speak louder to you than the voice of God. His Word is truth and life!

There are many voices to listen to,
To convince you it is not true.
So many voices,
That desire you to hear;
There are many voices that desire your ear.

To speak into your soul and mind,
And have you twisted all the time.
But there is One whom I know,
Who will speak truth to your mind,
will, and your emotions,
And answer all of your questions.

But there are those who seek to override you,
Remove what God hides in you,
And uproot the living truth,
Desiring to stamp out the light that shines within.
They are comfortable with sin.

When they speak, cast the words to their feet,
Recognize what you hear,
But do not allow it in your ear,
Because if you do,
Their words will molest you.

Like the devil molesting the mind of Eve,
How was she deceived?
When she knew what God had said.
Yet, the voice of another
Manipulated her instead.

Covering

Prelude

There is safety and security in being under the shadow of the Almighty. His covering protects, defends and shields you from the advancement of the adversary. Under His cover is peace and joy. He is reachable and His presence is tangible. You will find yourself not far from Him at all while abiding under His covering. In His presence is everything you need or could ask for. He possesses all that is and is always willing to supply your every need. He alone is the provider of every one of them. He is the only one who can satisfy them. God is our covering; no one has our best interest held in their heart like He does.

In the midst of moments when I cannot see,
I hear Your Words ringing out to me.
Your Words encouraging in my ear.
Your Words calming my silent fears.
"Believe Me," You say. "Just only believe."
I find myself safe in Your covering.

Like a cloak, I see You overshadow me,
As an oversized garment You spread like wings.
I can feel Your presence and in it I shrink.
It is so real, the tangibility of Your feel,
I feel Your breath, and I can breathe.
I find myself safe in Your covering.

Shaping me, molding me, aligning me to You.
Completing what You have longed to do.
I surrender to the desire of Your heart;
The fears I had no longer are.
You call me to a place of total trust,
To rest in the truth of Your magnificent love.

I find myself safe in Your covering.
I find myself safe in Your covering.
I find myself safe!

Freedom

Prelude

When God loves, in the purity of His love He recognizes our faults but sees beyond them into our needs. He sees the struggles, He sees the failures, He sees the weaknesses and He sees the helplessness and has compassion. God is paying attention to everything we do. He watches as we walk in disobedience. In our disobedience, He observes the birthing of our sin. As God witnesses our sin, He endures the heartache as He looks at his "children of disobedience" because He knows His own decree; the wages of our sin is death.

The heartache of God suffers long for a people that He loves and desires intimate relationship with. Yet He has chosen to love regardless of the offense. In love, He forgives us who simply come and ask for forgiveness. He holds no grudges. He denies not. He continues to love.

This is agape love. This is the love God has commanded you to share with people that hurt you, mistreated you, ridiculed you and despitefully used you. This love does not seek revenge or calculate the charges. It does not seek to satisfy itself. This love does not harbor contempt, or strife, nor does it harbor malice in the heart. It is love that loves completely.

The beauty of the agape love of God is His wonderful, precious benefits. We are liberated. We are freed by love to love. Love forgives! In forgiveness, your heart remains unbound to the offenses. So you remain free. Free to be whole and healthy as God intended.

However, this is a love in God apprehended through Christ Jesus. It is the Spirit of God that enables or undergirds us with the ability to love to such a complete degree. Without the Spirit of God, this love is unattainable.

God's love is complete, pure and undefiled.
He loves thoroughly, from beginning to end.
When we strike His heart with disobedience,
He is willing and ready to forgive, if we repent.

He doesn't dangle our mistreatment in our face,
He separates it as far as the east is from the west,
And remembers it not, He wipes the slate clean,
An opportune moment He graces us with again.

Agape love is pure love.
It is love that does not assault its offender.
It is love that lets go of the offense,
And frees the guilty of their charge.

It is a love of absolute forgiveness.
A love that does not recall into memory.
Some say, "I will forgive, but I will not forget.
Why remain a prisoner of your own mind?

This is not human love.
This is the love of God given to humanity!
It comes from God, given to you by His Spirit.
It is love that completely sets you free.

Watch Me

Prelude

Why is it that when we experience a situation in our life we tend to look at the situation instead of looking to God? We become fixated on the problem and begin to worry about what we see before us. We so quickly forget who God is and what He has done for us in the past. We lose our footing and ground in the kingdom because of what we see happening to us in the earth. But God is the same God today as He was yesterday. He changes not. If He saw you through something once, why would He not see you through it again and again and again? He covers us and He takes care of us. I know about fears and being frightened when situations have occurred in my life. Sometimes He has had to say, "What are you tripping on?" I know that is not good grammar! But sometimes He does! He asks, "Did I not see you through once? Why would you not trust Me? What is it for Me to see you through this? Move out of the way and give Me room to express Myself. Stand back and watch Me be God!"

Step back and watch Me perform.
What I said, I will do it!
Because I am the Lord.
As you look across your past,

The troubles seemed so vast.
Did I not bring you through?
Did I not do what I said I was going to?

I said I would never leave nor forsake you.
I would never abandon you,
Never leave you alone on your own.
Have I not been here for you?
Bending My ear to you?
Hearing you when you call out My name?

What has changed?
Surely it is not I.
You know that I change not.
As with the troubles of your past,
I saw you through them all.
And I will see you through these.
What are they for Me?

Stand back and watch Me perform.
Stand back and watch the Spirit of your God.

Wicked

Prelude

More and more you witness the rise of men against men. There are more killings, maiming, and more destruction occurring. There is the self-indulged destruction one inflicts upon self; pharmaceuticals, whether legal or illegal. Where is self-restraint? Where is self-control? It is dissipating at a rapid speed as the hearts of men grow weary. I see the more God is denounced, the more evil is prevalent. It does not diminish God. However; it makes room for godless things to incubate more rapidly.

God is God! If you do not want God, He will not force Himself upon you. You must invite God into your life in order for Him to help you with your life. It appears that men are more willing to do evil and are glad to accommodate, rather than stand up for what is good and righteous. Pray for our country; we are in desperate need of it. Pray for the world!

I heard of these days coming.
Not only do I see them approaching,
But I see them running and positioning themselves.

I behold the captured minds of men,
Tripping over their own thoughts,
Like drunk men staggering.

They believe according to their own interpretations,
Their feet follow whatever is in their minds.
Their hands yield to whatever delights them.

It is like a sickness, a disease.
It is spreading so quickly,
And it is without regret.

Their hearts are given over to themselves,
Such a deceitful and wicked instrument,
They do what is unseemly.

Unaware that the very things that are chosen,
Shall appear to testify for or against them,
On the day men's testimony is required.

For they have lost their discernment
between good and evil,
And it has estranged their relationship
with the true and living God.
But they perceive it not.

Their lips attempt to speak of Him,
But their soul is shrouded in darkness.
Oh, how man has deceived himself!

And how quickly he runs and gladly does evil.
What shall become of men in the
day of their judgment?
What shall become of the deceptive minds of men?

I Found Love

Prelude

Relationships are interesting. You desire to give love as well as receive love. When this does not occur, you are dissatisfied in the relationship. You need the expression of love to be reciprocated. You find yourself lonely, needing and disconnected, even though you are in relationship with the person you love. I asked God, "Is there someone who can love me the way You know I need love? Is there someone you have for me?" When I asked God those questions, He began to focus my attention on Him and His love for me. As I learned His heart for mine, I discovered His love superseded all other love. There is no other relationship that satisfies my soul.

I used to look around,
For the love that could not be found.
You see,
No one cared for me,
The way my heart needed to be.
And then, I saw my Father,
Who superseded all love,
He superseded all joy,
He superseded all peace of mind.

I used to ask the Lord,
Is there anyone You've prepared for me?
Who can love my heart tenderly?
God, You know how You created me.
And I saw my Father,
Who superseded all love,
Who superseded all joy,
Who superseded all peace of mind.

I saw the Lord.
He beckoned me to come.
He said, "Sit with Me for a while.
I'm the One you're looking for, My child.
I am your Father,
I supersede all love,
I supersede all joy,
I supersede all peace of mind."

As God began to share His heart,
My mind was overwhelmed,
Gasping for an understanding,
At the insurmountable measure of His love.
I could see that my Father,
Supersedes all love,
Supersedes all joy,
Supersedes all peace of mind.

I stopped looking...

Intimacy

Prelude

God has a passionate desire for us to individually know Him. To know Him is to spend time with Him. We need to spend time with Him in His Word and in prayer. God loves sharing His heart. Who is better at explaining God to you than God clarifying Himself? When I heard this song in my spirit as I stood in my kitchen, I stood motionless in amazement. I could not believe that God would call me into such a gratifying relationship with Him. Sure, I heard of pastors, preachers and evangelists describing relationships with God that were phenomenal. But I heard God sing this song to me! I have learned that the more time I spend with God, the more He describes Himself. I have also come to understand there is so much more about God I do not know. In time, I am confident He will ensure I understand as I deliberately pursue the knowledge of Him.

I don't want you to know man's interpretation,
I want you to know My revelation.
Who has sat in the council of My will,
That they can speak My mind?

The spirit of a man only knows the spirit of a man,
But the Spirit of God the things which are God's.
And those that sit in the council of My will,
To them I reveal My heart, I make it known.

But how can you hear if you are not listening?
How can you listen if you're absent from My throne?
And how can you be absent and say
you know what I am saying,
When you haven't spent any time with Me to know?

I desire relationship with you,
To speak My Words of wisdom into your soul,
And open your heart so that I may enter in,
And unveil My heart before your own.

Intimacy brings forth revelation.
In My presence I make Myself known.
Revealing to you the mysteries of My kingdom,
So you can speak what I have spoken.

How can you hear if you are not listening?
How can you listen if you are
absent from My throne?
How can you be absent and say you
know what I am saying,
When you haven't spent any time with Me to know?

Secret Place

Prelude

When there is no one else in the world that cares or desires to listen to you, God is always here. He is always present. He is always in your right-now moment. No matter what you desire to communicate to Him or talk to Him about. He is always willing to hear what you need to say. He can hear your spoken words as well as the ones you are incapable of verbally uttering. He desires to hear from you. He desires you come to Him and share your heart. God is always available. He is more than willing and able to do great and marvelous things on your behalf. There is no better place than in the secret place of His presence. There is no substitute!

In my moment of silence,
I am still within myself.
With so much to say,
Yet saying nothing.

In my solemn existence,
My heart yearns to speak.
I beckon for an ear.
But there is none to hear.

I run to my secret place,
Where every word from my lips is heard,
Every tear from my eye is noticed,
And where peace lifts and embraces me.

I hear Your voice say,
"Here am I.
From heaven I bend My ear,
I see thy tears.

I am Your comfort,
And you are My love.
I am Your way-maker,
And you are My song.

For in Me you have discovered
That I am like no other one.
Run, run to Me,
For I am Your secret place."

Shape Me

Prelude

Without the earnest desire to become the image of Christ, the walk with God will be an estranged one. It will be difficult to reproduce the attributes of Christ without the will to be like Him. It is the life of Christ we are to duplicate. It isn't always easy, and we sometimes miss the mark. Remember the passage in the scriptures, "We have all fallen short." But still, we are to strive to become like Jesus Christ. He is our example. We cannot live according to our own passions; we must surrender ourselves to the Spirit of God and be conformed into the image of His Son. This psalm is asking for God to transform me. I do not know about you, but I need God to change me completely!

Make me into the image of Thy Son.
There is a race I have to run.
Take me,
Pour in me Thy will.
As I stand here waiting … fill.

I want to do what You want,
Be what You need,
I want to finish my course please!
I need Your strength to go on,
Your power to be strong.

I need Your presence with me every day,
Your Spirit to lead me in Thy ways.
I need to walk by Your side.
In the cool of the day,
And in the middle of the night.

Bless me with both Your will and desire to do.
Surrender what You require me to.
Submit to You my all,
Quickly respond whenever You call,
I do not want to hesitate or procrastinate.

Make me into the image of Thy Son.
There is a race I must run until I'm done.

Recognition

Prelude

It is amazing when God begins to ask you questions regarding Him. It illustrates His grace, mercy and love when He brings Himself to your attention. He does it for the benefit of you and me. He knows who He is! But sometimes we forget. When that happens He is merciful enough to help us regain our perspective. We are so needy. At least I know I am. If God did not communicate and explain things about Himself, how could my mind and heart ever capture Him? Not that I have. It is a major difference when God shows or tells you something opposed to when you hear it from someone else. I just think it is so awesome that He would desire to tell us anything about Himself. He doesn't have to, but He does so that we may acquire an intense comprehension of His desires. I am always wowed!

Do you see Me for who I am when
you come before Me?
Do you understand you are standing in the
presence of the God of all creation?
The God that holds the keys of life and
death in the palm of His hand,
The God that contains every answer to
every question your mind can conceive.

The God that can deliver every
miracle you can believe for,
Standing ready to release the manifestation
of such divine substance.

The God that possesses every treasure,
every precious and good thing,
The God who forever, eternally loves you and
desires to make Himself to shine upon you,
The God who desires to passionately overtake
you by the power of His intense love,
Do you recognize My kindness, My grace, My
goodness, My forgiveness, My mercy, My love!
Do you see Me? Do you really?

Creative Power

Prelude

Do you ever think about the power of God's Word? God spoke all that is into existence. Except man, He created him with His own hands. The creative power of His Word manifested what He spoke. What was in the mind of God appeared.

Imagine God speaking light and light was! God's Word has unimaginable creative power. When He speaks, He can cause things to happen or become. God spoke to the earth to bring forth living creatures after their kind and it was so. His Word contained everything in it to cause the earth to form what his Word demanded it to create. These creatures came up and out from the earth perfectly formed with everything necessary for them to flourish and succeed. God's Word is alive! God's Word is life! God's Word is spirit, capable and more than able to perform what God launches it to accomplish to the finish.

If God's Word can create the heavens and the earth, and by what is manifested we can behold the works of His glory, why would we find it difficult to believe His "words of promise" that He has spoken to us?

When we open our eyes, is it not obvious that we see Him in His creation everywhere? He testifies of Himself in everything He has created and in everything He has made. Yet, we have trouble believing

Him for the "words of life" He has given to us. Why would He not do what He has said to you and me? We must dare to believe Him! His "words of promise" are *yea* and *amen*. He is not a man. He is God and He cannot lie! We must believe Him at His Word.

I can call anything into existence,
I can create anything!
Whatever I say it becomes.
Whatever I declare it shall be.

My Word created all you behold.
My Word formed and made it all!
And without my Word no-thing could exist.
Still, all is sustained and upheld, yes! By my Word.

I have covenant with the sun and the moon.
They agree to perform rotation of times.
I bless the earth with all that is good.
And provide seasons for the inhabitants in it.

When I said, "Let there become," it still is.
Has creation ceased creating?
Has man stopped populating?
No, these things continue to occur because of Me!

I am God!
No one has done this but I.
No one can be credited except Me.
Because I Am the One who has
done such wondrous things.

You Take My Breath Away

Prelude

There is nothing like being in the presence of God. Sometimes His presence is too much for me to embrace. He has to touch me with His peace; if He did not, I would not be able to stand. In His presence His love is so overwhelming. I am lost in the moment and nothing seems to exist except the two of us. He is so wonderful. There are times in His presence, He takes my breath away, and in those moments I can hardly breathe.

In Your presence,
There is glory.
I fall down and bow before You on my knees.
Here I worship,
My heart surrenders,
I am lost to only find You next to me.
You take my breath away,
You take my breath away,
I can hardly breathe, breathe in me.

In Your presence,
There is goodness.

I see Your mercy dancing all around me.
So I trust You,
My soul believes,
You have shown me love that I have never seen.
You take my breath away.
You take my breath away.
I can hardly breathe, breathe in me.

In Your presence,
There is peace.
You overcome every one of my fears.
So I rest in You;
I let myself go.
In the safety of Your arms You carry me.
You take my breath away.
You take my breath away.
I can hardly breathe, breathe in me.
'Cause You take my breath away…

God's Decision

Prelude

God hears and answers prayers. He said, if you pray believing and not pray amiss, He will hear and answer you. When it does not appear as though God has heard your cry, He has. Sometimes He answers with a response you were not expecting, but He still answered. In situations when you do not understand what He has done or why He has done it, you must trust Him. I heard a Bishop speak at a conference and say, "Understanding was not a prerequisite for obedience." Understanding everything that God does is not a prerequisite for trusting Him either. You must trust Him even when you cannot understand anything at all.

The Word of God teaches that He works everything out for our good. At times we question, how can this be good when the suffering and the pain is so devastating? How do you catch your breath when the hurt is so overwhelming and the blow has knocked the wind of life out of you? God knows better than we. How can the created know the mind of the Creator, as though we have that ability? We do not. Whatever happens in our lives, whatever hurts, pains, sufferings and disappointments, we still must trust God. He is the only One who can and will see us through all things and comfort us in the midst of what we cannot comprehend.

In memory of Pastor Elvia Cardoso

I prayed for you,
I believed God with you,
I anticipated and expected your miracle,
But God chose to answer you in His own way,
Contrary to what I had hoped for and believed.

I do not understand!
Because I know God heard my cries on your behalf,
I know that God is the God of the miraculous,
I still know that He is,
So I must trust in God's decision for you.
I must trust what He has chosen.

It doesn't seem real,
But you are not here,
So you must be standing in the presence of God,
Kissing on the Master's cheeks,
And lying at His feet,
And worshipping Him.

Now you abide in eternity,
Where sickness has no place,
Where dancing and praising God never ceases,
And the joy of the Lord is a forever flowing fountain.
Your smile now lights up the heavens,
And on the earth, the light of
your smile is seen missing.

The Finish Line

Prelude

Death is a sure thing. It is the one thing in life we can count on because it is inevitable. The Word of God informs us that it is appointed for men to die once and then there is judgment. God created time but is not subjected to time. We live in time and God exists outside of it. When it is one of our loved one's time to ascend to the heavens, we find ourselves heartbroken and rightfully so. No one desires to live without the touch, the sound and the passion of the one traveling onward from this realm to the next. In this we grieve due to the absence of one remembered.

My heart cries as I remember my uncle, Superintendent John L. Ganaway. He evangelized and preached the gospel of Jesus Christ for as long as I knew him. He was a pastor, a preacher, an evangelist, a husband, a father, a brother and great uncle. The Lord saw fit to give him eighty-two years before He sent the angels to escort him home. Sometimes it is unbelievable when you see people leave. Nevertheless, it is what it is, and you and I must embrace that heartbreaking reality. In the early morning on the day of his home going, I was considering his life. God put what I am about to share with you in my mind. It was a great comfort to my heart, although I could only imagine this occurring. It made me realize when you have finished your course, there is nothing left for you to fulfill. You are ready for the finish line. The power of God is so awesome because God truly is a comforter amidst tragedy and heartache.

In memory of Superintendent John L. Ganaway

I could only imagine,
As he saw the "Angels of the Lord"
Approaching him on behalf of God,
That he considered his life and saw,
Through the good and the bad,
Through the circumstances he had,
He saw God was with him.
I could only imagine he said,
"I fought good!
I fought real, real good!
I fought a good fight,
And I fought on the winning side."

I could only imagine, as he heard
the "Footsteps of the Lord,"
Sounding closer to his door,
He reviewed the things of God,
The things God birthed in his spirit.
He saw he had fulfilled God's will,
Nothing left undone here.
I could only imagine he said,
"I have accomplished my course.
I have satisfied You, my Lord.
I have done what You have asked.
Nothing more, there's nothing else left."

I could only imagine,
As the "Wings of the Angels,"
Spread to escort him to the King of Kings,
I could hear him sing,
"Sometimes it was hard,
But I stayed with You, God.
I didn't lose my place in the race.
You see I have kept the faith.
I can only imagine him saying,
"Therefore into Your arms I come,
Into Your arms I run, run, run,
I cross the *finish line.*

Divine Beauty

How do we see one another? What do you notice when you look into the life of someone else, when you take a moment to become absent in the observation of your own? When you look, when you take note, when you minimally observe, do you acknowledge the faults of one's humanity? Or can you recognize the divine beauty God has created in them?

Divine beauty is the truth and essence of who we truly are, the beautiful one God created us to be. Unfortunately, we do not always live in that truth; many times we live beneath the truth for whatever reason—whether we don't believe the truth, have low self-esteem, or were told by someone we would simply never amount to anything. But God created us divinely beautiful!

In His image He created you and me lovely. We are the workmanship of his hands! If you take a moment, you will see divine beauty in the lives of many. It is not without faults, no, no; but in spite of someone's faults, you recognize the beauty that God has divinely placed in them. Sometimes people miss seeing beauty within them and need to be aimed, aligned, and adjusted by the simple usage of some enlightening, thought-provoking words that stir up and elevate the soul to unrealized heights.

A simple conversation has the potential to prick the mind of a person and stir their heart to discover what God has ordained for their life. The power of a simple human experience through words is priceless, even if those words are spoken by a stranger. You say, "That is all hogwash." No, it isn't because it happened to me. There was someone that I didn't know, who shared their thoughts regarding what they saw in me as a young woman. I have never forgotten that experience to this day. I have not forgotten the person, nor have I forgotten the words that were spoken to me. One day long ago, I sat in a restaurant and a stranger asked if they could sit with me. What this person had spoken to me were words I had never considered before, but they changed my life forever.

It is always incredible how one can see greatness in someone who cannot oftentimes see it in themselves. It is amazing how words can illuminate one's mind to see things they have never seen and dream what they have never dreamed.

When was the last time you spoke into the life of someone, something you saw that they had not yet discovered? Have you recognized divine beauty in anyone lately, or do you only see his or her human frailties?

Wisdoms in Short Form

Strong

In the face of adversity, one must press against the odds, taking by force the territory God has given you. Take it little by little, until you have overcome all the obstacles and come into the place of your possession.

Stability

Stability is anchored and solidified in the endless counsel of God. In His counsel you find soundness and grounding. For it is the thing that illuminates the placement of your feet, to identify where you stand; it reveals your heart and transforms your mind that life may be lived at a greater level in the unfathomable riches in the abundance of God.

Calm

It is the position or state of one who is untroubled. It is a place where the undisturbed is seated and resting in God. It is a state where you are not moved by issues or circumstances because of your trust in God. It is peace, the kind Christ has left with you.

Faith

Faith is seeing beyond what your natural eyes behold and piercing in the sphere of the supernatural truth, taking hold of that truth to possess the realities of God.

Perseverance

Perseverance is the constant hot pursuit of your dream, your vision. It is the never-ending force that propels you into your destiny. It is never quitting and never surrendering to anything less than what God has birthed in you and offers nothing short of obtained success.

Trust

Trust is the consuming force on which belief rides, doubting nothing in God, only being overwhelmed and thoroughly convinced that God is in total control. Knowing God will perform what He sent His Word out to do.

Book Summary

Take the time to spend time with God. It is only in spending time with Him that you will come into the most intimate and relevant relationship you have ever known. You will come to know who He is by His revelation of Himself. It is wonderful, mystical and sometimes inexplicable—that's just how God is. You will experience an incredible love affair and begin to learn about the passion He possesses for your soul. His love is relentless at elevating you to greater heights and depths in who He truly is, illuminating your understanding then adding to it. He will cover you, comfort you and be there for you no matter what. When you can't find anyone to talk to or share your heart with, He is here to hear your every word and have a solution that is beneficial for your life.

God is so beautiful! He loves us beyond the expression of words. He manifested His love by the birth, death, and resurrection of His Son, Christ Jesus, which gave all of us an avenue of return into right relationship with God through the Lord: Jesus Christ. God's heartfelt desire is for His creation to know Him and know who they are in Him. He wants our lives to be blessed, supernaturally blessed, through relationship and obedience to His will, which is demonstrated in His Word. It is God who has drawn me into a mind-blowing, heartfelt, intimate relationship with Him. I did not run after Him. He came after me.

But doesn't His love run after all of us? His relationship with me affords this writer the humble opportunity to write this "situational poetic" book, *From the Father's Heart*.